HOW TO LEARN BASIC BOOKKEEPING IN TEN EASY LESSONS

John Barnes

HOW TO LEARN BASIC BOOKKEEPING IN TEN EASY LESSONS

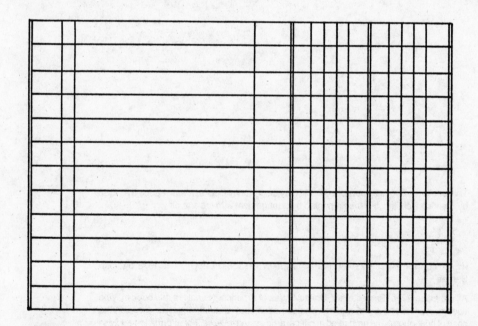

BARNES & NOBLE BOOKS
A DIVISION OF HARPER & ROW, PUBLISHERS

New York, Cambridge, Philadelphia, San Francisco, Washington
London, Mexico City, São Paulo, Singapore, Sydney

To the many wonderful,
wonderful students who,
over the years, said:
"Mr Barnes, why don't you
write your own book?"
Thanks for your inspiration
and encouragement.
and _____
To Cathy

This book was originally published in 1978 by Opportunity Books. It was reprinted in 1982 by Prentice-Hall, Inc. It is here reprinted by arrangement with the author.

HOW TO LEARN BASIC BOOKKEEPING IN TEN EASY LESSONS. Copyright © 1978 by John Barnes

First BARNES & NOBLE edition published 1987.

LIBRARY OF CONGRESS CATALOG CARD NUMBER: 86-45638

ISBN: 0-06-463721-2

92 93 94 95 MPC 10 9 8 7 6

CONTENTS

FOREWORD

There are a great many bookkeeping and accounting systems in general use, each adapted to the peculiar needs and requirements of the business using it. However, all systems are based on accepted bookkeeping and accounting principles developed and refined over the years.

Here, for the first time, these principles are presented in such a crystal clear and concise manner that almost anyone with a simple will to learn can grasp their meaning and understand them.

The unique methods used to introduce and explain the traditional bookkeeping and accounting principles evolved from hundreds of hours of actual classroom instruction by the author to a countless number of students during the past 28 years.

The Three Simplified Rules, developed by the author and found in no other book, insure that almost anyone who can read can learn basic bookkeeping.

Whether you are interested in acquiring the necessary knowledge and skills that will enable you to enter the lucrative field of bookkeeping and accounting; whether you are in business for yourself and wish to learn how to keep the books for your own business; whether your present position would be enhanced if you knew how to review and interpret bookkeeping records; or whether you might wish to go into business for yourself by opening a profitable bookkeeping service right in your own home—you will find this book will easily and surely lead you to the attainment of your goal.

LESSON ONE

Ledger Accounts; Debits and Credits

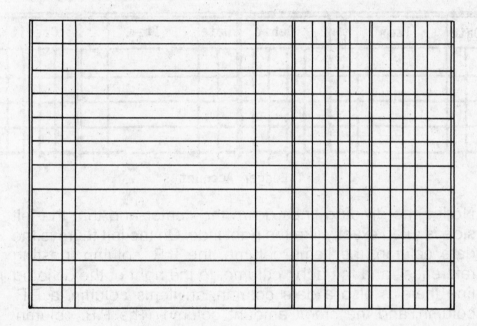

The two main types of records used in bookkeeping are *journals* and *ledgers.* The journal is commonly called the "book of original entry" because transactions are always recorded first of all in a journal and then, from time to time, are posted—or transferred—to the ledger accounts.

Although the journal is the book of original entry, in studying bookkeeping we take up the ledger first because it is easier to learn the principle of debits and credits by working with ledger accounts. Once you have learned this, you will easily understand how to use the journal.

A ledger account is often called a T ledger account because it is in the shape of a large T.

Date	Item	P. R.	Debit	Date	Item	P. R.	Credit

T Ledger Account

Notice the dividing lines down the center and that the left side is ruled exactly like the right side. On the left there is the date column, the items column, the P.R. column (posting reference), and the debit column; to the right of the dividing line there is also a date column, an items column, a P.R. column, and the credit amount column. (The P.R. column, which means Posting Reference column, will not be used at present and will be explained fully in a later chapter.)

DEBIT SIDE AND CREDIT SIDE

In referring to a ledger account we do not say left side and right side, but instead we say debit side and credit side. The left side is called the debit side and the right side is called the credit side. You will note that as applied to a T ledger account the words *debit* and *credit* do not have their usual meanings. We are accustomed to thinking of an insurance man who has a debit he collects, or we say we have credit at a store or at the bank. We need to forget the usual connotations of these words and to remember that the ONLY thing debit means is the *left-hand side of a T ledger account,* and the ONLY thing credit means is the *right-hand side of a T ledger account.* To help you remember which comes first, just think of Washington, D. C. *D.C.—debit and credit.* Abbreviations are also commonly used for these two words: Dr. for debit, and Cr. for credit. Once again, Dr. or debit means the left-hand side, and Cr. or credit means the right-hand side.

Now let's look at three typical ledger accounts with some figures already entered in them. We have simply drawn three ledger accounts, omitting some of the lines and the date column, but you note they are still in the shape of a large T. The left side is the debit side (Dr.) and the right side is the credit side (Cr.).

Dr.		Cash	Cr.	
Jan. 1	100	Jan. 5	200
2	250	8	45
3	75		

Dr.		Office Equipment	Cr.
Jan. 5	500		
8	350		

Dr.		Rent Expense	Cr.
Jan. 1	800		

ACCOUNTING TERMS

Referring to the above ledger accounts, here are some of the accounting terms we use. We say the Cash account has three debit entries in it, and it has two credit entries in it. (Meaning, of course, that there are three entries on the left side and two entries on the right side.) Or, we say on Jan. 1 we debited Cash for $100, on Jan. 2 we debited Cash for $250, on Jan. 3 we debited Cash for $75. On Jan. 5 we credited Cash for $200 and on Jan. 8 we credited Cash for $45. Debit Cash means to enter the amount on the left side of Cash; credit Cash means to enter the amount on the right side of Cash.

Looking at the Office Equipment account, you note on Jan. 5 we debited it for $500, and on Jan. 8 we debited it for $350. Looking at the Rent Expense account, you note on Jan. 1 we debited it for $800.

Read the above again and *refer to the T ledger accounts as you read.* You should now understand that debiting any account simply means writing the amount on the left side of the account; crediting any account simply means writing the amount on the right side of the account. Note that it is customary to omit the dollar sign ($) when figures are entered in the ledger accounts. (Sometimes the word *charge* is used in place of *debit. Charging* an account means *debiting* the account.)

THE THREE KINDS OF LEDGER ACCOUNTS

There is a ledger account for each type of transaction that occurs in the business. There may be fifty or sixty different accounts in the ledger; for example, there is one for Cash, one for Equipment, one for Accounts Payable, one for Rent Expense, one for Income From Fees, etc. However, the accounts are divided into three kinds, or groups. The three kinds of accounts are: *asset accounts, liability accounts,* and *owner's equity accounts.* Next we will define each of these three kinds of accounts and give one or two examples of each.

1. An *asset* is anything of value owned by the business.
   Example Cash and Equipment

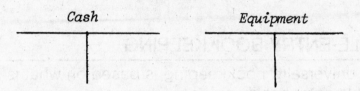

2. A *liability* is a debt, or something we owe.
   Example Accounts Payable

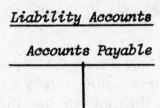

3. *Owner's equity* means the owner's net worth or capital.
   Example Income From Fees and Rent Expense

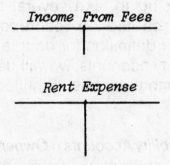

Since Cash and Equipment are each things of value they belong to the *asset* group of accounts.

Since Accounts Payable is the account that deals with what we owe, it belongs to the *liability* group of accounts.

Any account that affects—that is, either increases or decreases—the owner's net worth belongs to the *Owner's Equity* group of accounts. Since Income From Fees affects the owner's equity (increases it) and Rent Expense affects the owner's equity (decreases it), both of these accounts belong to the *Owner's Equity* group.

DOUBLE-ENTRY BOOKKEEPING

Almost universally, bookkeeping is based on what is known as *double-entry bookkeeping.*

DOUBLE-ENTRY BOOKKEEPING MEANS THAT EACH TRANS- ACTION AFFECTS TWO OF THE T LEDGER ACCOUNTS, AND WE MUST DEBIT ONE OF THOSE ACCOUNTS AND CREDIT THE OTHER ONE.

By the word *transaction* we mean any economic event that causes an exchange of value. It refers to any event or happening that occurs throughout the business day that requires the bookkeeper to make an entry in the books. For example, buying equipment, buying merchandise, selling merchandise, paying rent for the month, paying salaries, etc., are all *transactions,* and each affects two ledger accounts— and we must debit one of these accounts and credit the other one.

Next we are going to take several typical transactions and see how they should be recorded in the ledger accounts, applying our definition for double-entry bookkeeping. Instead of fifty or sixty accounts, we will use just five accounts to start with. Notice that each is identified as to what kind of account it is.

Asset Accounts	*Liability Accounts*	*Owner's Equity*
1. Cash	3. Accounts	4. Income From Fees
2. Equipment	Payable	5. Rent Expense

Note that each of the following transactions affects *two* of the above accounts and that we *debit* one of those accounts and *credit* the other one.

A. *Bought equipment for cash, $500* (Notice this affects two accounts, Equipment and Cash. We debit Equipment and credit Cash)

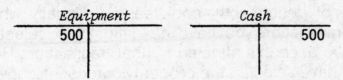

Equipment		Cash	
500			500

B. *Bought equipment on credit, or on account, $100* (Notice this affects two accounts, Equipment and Accounts Payable. We debit Equipment and credit Accounts Payable)

Equipment		Accounts Payable	
100			100

C. *Paid rent for one month, $600* (Notice this affects two accounts, Rent Expense and Cash. We debit Rent Expense and credit Cash)

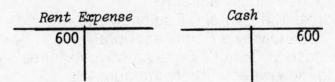

Rent Expense		Cash	
600			600

D. *Received a $50 fee for services* (Notice this affects two accounts, Cash and Income From Fees. We debit Cash and credit Income From Fees)

Cash		Income From Fees	
50			50

WHICH ACCOUNT SHOULD BE DEBITED AND WHICH ACCOUNT SHOULD BE CREDITED?

The above graphically illustrates exactly how we apply the principle of double-entry bookkeeping. Usually when you read a transaction you have no difficulty in selecting the proper two accounts affected by that transaction. However, once we have selected the proper two accounts, *how do we know which of the two should be debited and which should be credited?* This brings us to the Six Fundamental Bookkeeping Rules or principles that tell us exactly which account should be debited and which account should be credited.

Six Fundamental Bookkeeping Rules

1. An increase in an Asset account always requires a debit entry to the Asset account.
2. A decrease in an Asset account always requires a credit entry to the Asset account.
3. An increase in a Liability account always requires a credit entry to the Liability account.
4. A decrease in a Liability account always requires a debit entry to the Liability account.
5. An increase in Owner's Equity always requires a credit entry to the Owner's Equity account.
6. A decrease in Owner's Equity always requires a debit entry to the Owner's Equity account.

Here is how you can learn the six rules in two or three minutes. Note that Rules 3 and 4 for Liability accounts and Rules 5 and 6 for Owner's Equity accounts are exactly the same, and they are just the opposite of Rules 1 and 2 for Asset accounts. Therefore, if you learn the first two you know all six, because the others are just the opposite of the first two. As we explain how to use the rules, keep referring to them until you have had a chance to memorize them.

Next we will take up several transactions and illustrate and explain in detail exactly how to use the six fundamental bookkeeping rules.

Note: *Once we complete this, we are immediately going to give you Three Simplified Rules which will show you how to record easily about* 90 percent of all transactions that occur in basic bookkeeping. *Study the following carefully and learn it, but remember we are immediately going to reduce the six rules to Three Simplified Rules.*

Here are the six rules again so you won't have to keep turning back:

1. An increase in an Asset always requires a debit entry.
2. A decrease in an Asset always requires a credit entry.
3. An increase in a Liability always requires a credit entry.
4. A decrease in a Liability always requires a debit entry.
5. An increase in Owner's Equity always requires a credit entry.
6. A decrease in Owner's Equity always requires a debit entry.

Asset Accounts	*Liability Accounts*	*Owner's Equity*
1. Cash	3. Accounts	4. Income From Fees
2. Equipment	Payable	5. Rent Expense

Remember, each transaction affects two of the above accounts, and we will debit one and credit the other, using the six fundamental rules.

A. *Bought equipment for cash, $500*

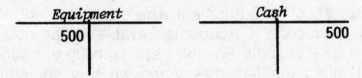

Look at the five accounts listed above. This transaction affects two of those accounts, Cash and Equipment. Let's consider the Equipment account first. What kind of account is Equipment? It is an Asset account. When we buy Equipment, are we increasing or decreasing the asset Equipment? We are *increasing* it, for we now have more equipment than we had before. *Look at Rule 1.* It says *an increase in an Asset always requires a debit entry,* therefore we debit the Asset account, Equipment. Now consider the other account affected by this transaction, Cash. What kind of account is

Cash? It is also an Asset account. When we pay out $500 how does that affect the asset Cash? It *decreases* it. *Look at Rule 2.* It says *a decrease in an Asset always requires a credit entry*, therefore we credit the Asset account, Cash.

ANALYZING

We are going to take each transaction and analyze it in this same manner: 1. Read the transaction. 2. Decide which two accounts are affected. 3. Take one of those accounts and decide what kind of account it is. 4. Decide if it is being increased or decreased. 5. Select the correct one of the six rules that applies to that situation and do what it says.

B. Bought equipment on credit, or on account, $100

Equipment	Accounts Payable
100	100

What two accounts are affected by this transaction? The two accounts are *Equipment* and *Accounts Payable*. Equipment is an Asset. When we buy more equipment we are increasing the Asset, Equipment. *Look at Rule 1.* It says *an increase in an Asset always requires a debit entry;* therefore, we debit the Asset account, Equipment. The other account affected by this transaction is Accounts Payable. What kind of account is it? Accounts Payable is a Liability account. How does it affect our liabilities when we buy something on account. It *increases* them, for we now owe more than we did before. Look at Rule 3. It says *an increase in a Liability always requires a credit entry*; therefore, we credit the Liability account, Accounts Payable.

C. Paid rent for one month, $600

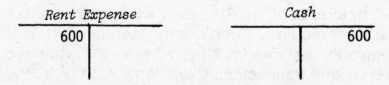

Rent Expense	Cash
600	600

What two accounts are affected by this transaction? The two accounts are *Rent Expense* and *Cash.* What kind of account is Rent Expense? It is an Owner's Equity account. Does paying rent for the month increase or decrease the Owner's Equity, or net worth? It decreases it. Look at Rule 6. It says *a decrease in Owner's Equity always requires a debit entry*; therefore, we debit the Owner's Equity account, Rent Expense. The other account affected by this transaction is Cash. Cash is an Asset. When we pay out $600, we decrease the Asset, Cash. Look at Rule 2. It says *a decrease in an Asset always requires a credit entry*; therefore, we credit the Asset account, Cash.

D. *Received a $50 fee for services*

Cash		Income From Fees	
50			50

What two accounts are affected? The two accounts are *Cash* and *Income From Fees.* What kind of account is Cash? Cash is an Asset account. When we receive money, we are increasing the Asset, Cash. Look at Rule 1. It says *an increase in an Asset always requires a debit entry*; therefore, we debit the Asset account, Cash. The other account affected is Income From Fees. What kind of account is it? Income From Fees is an Owner's Equity account. When we receive a $50 fee, we are increasing the owner's equity, or net worth. Look at Rule 5. It says *an increase in Owner's Equity always requires a credit entry*; therefore, we credit the Owner's Equity account, Income From Fees.

E. *Paid $75 on account*

Cash		Accounts Payable	
	75	75	

What two accounts are affected? The two accounts are *Cash* and *Accounts Payable.* Cash is an Asset account. When we pay $75, we are decreasing the Asset, Cash. Look at Rule 2. It says *a decrease in an Asset always requires a credit entry*; therefore, we credit the Asset account, Cash. The other account affected is Accounts Payable. What kind of account is it? Accounts Payable is a Liability account. When we pay $75 on account, we decrease our liabilities, for we now owe $75 less. Look at Rule 4. It says *a decrease in a Liability always requires a debit entry*; therefore, we debit the Liability account, Accounts Payable.

The Three Simplified Rules

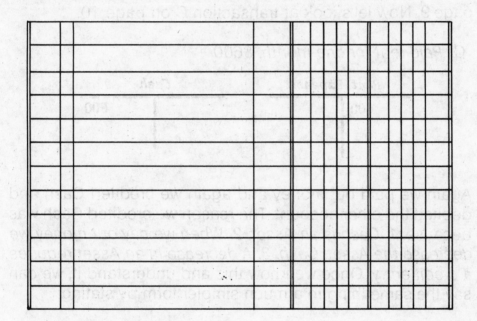

In Lesson One we stated that once we learned how to use and apply the Six Fundamental Bookkeeping Rules we were going to reduce them to *Three Simplified Rules*. Let's look again at transaction A on page 9.

A. *Bought equipment for cash, $500*

Equipment		Cash	
500			500

In this transaction we paid out money, so we credited Cash and debited the other account, for the reason given on page 9. Now let's look at transaction C on page 10.

C. *Paid rent for one month, $600*

Rent Expense		Cash	
600			600

Again we paid out money and again we credited Cash and debited the other account. The reason we credited Cash was because: *1. Cash is an Asset. 2. When we pay out money we decrease the Asset, Cash. 3. A decrease in an Asset requires a credit entry.* Once we know this and understand it, we can say the same thing in a much simpler form by stating:

WHENEVER WE PAY OUT MONEY, ALWAYS CREDIT CASH AND DEBIT THE OTHER ACCOUNT.

Next, let's look at transaction D on page 11.

D. *Received a $50 fee for services*

Cash		Income From Fees	
50			50

In this transaction we received money, so we debited Cash and credited the other account. The reason we debited Cash was because: *1. Cash is an Asset. 2. When we receive money we are increasing the Asset, Cash. 3. An increase in an Asset requires a debit entry.* We can restate this in simpler form by saying:

WHENEVER WE RECEIVE MONEY, ALWAYS DEBIT CASH AND CREDIT THE OTHER ACCOUNT.

Now let's look at transaction B on page 10.

B. Bought equipment on credit, or on account, $100

Equipment	Accounts Payable
100	100

In this transaction we bought equipment on account. Since we neither received any money nor paid out any money, this transaction does not affect the Cash account. It does affect *Equipment* and *Accounts Payable,* and we debit Equipment and credit Accounts Payable for the reasons given on page 9. For our third Simplified Rule we will just memorize the following:

WHENEVER WE BUY EQUIPMENT ON ACCOUNT ALWAYS DEBIT EQUIPMENT AND CREDIT ACCOUNTS PAYABLE.

So here are our three new simplified rules. Remember, they are not contrary to, and do not change the Six Fundamental Bookkeeping Rules. They merely restate the six rules in simplified form.

The Three Simplified Rules

1. Whenever we pay out money, *always* credit Cash and debit the other account.
2. Whenever we receive money, *always* debit Cash and credit the other account.
3. Whenever we buy equipment on account, *always* debit Equipment and credit Accounts Payable.

These simplified rules will hold true—and serve you well—no matter how high you go in studying bookkeeping and accounting. Remember, these rules are based on the Six Fundamental Bookkeeping principles; however, the simplified form of the rules will show you how to record—very easily and quickly—a large percentage of all the transactions you will ever encounter.

Study the Three Simplified Rules and learn them well. From now on, whenever you see the word *paid,* you should automatically, and rather unconsciously, know you are going to credit cash and debit the other account. When you see the words *received money*, you will automatically debit Cash and credit the other account.

One way to help you visualize this and remember it is to think of money as moving from left to right, in this manner:

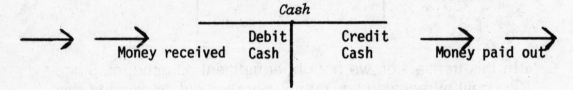

You will simply need to memorize Rule 3: Whenever we buy equipment on account, always debit Equipment and credit Accounts Payable.

APPLICATION OF THREE SIMPLIFIED RULES

We are now going to record the same five transactions once again, but this time we will use the Three Simplified Rules.

1. Whenever we pay out money, always credit Cash and debit the other account.
2. Whenever we receive money, always debit Cash and credit the other account.
3. Whenever we buy equipment on account, always debit Equipment and credit Accounts Payable.

A. *Bought equipment for cash, $500*

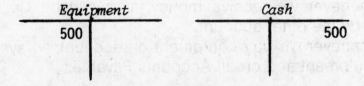

The two accounts affected are Equipment and Cash. Did we receive money or did we pay out money? We paid out money, so we use Simplified Rule 1, *Credit Cash and debit the other account.*

B. *Bought equipment on credit, or on account, $100*

Equipment	Accounts Payable
100	100

The two accounts affected are Equipment and Accounts Payable. We did not receive money, nor did we pay out money. We follow Simplified Rule 3, so we *debit Equipment and credit Accounts Payable.*

C. *Paid rent for one month, $600*

Rent Expense	Cash
600	600

The two accounts affected are Rent Expense and Cash. Did we receive money or did we pay out money? We paid out money, so we use Simplified Rule 1, *Credit Cash and debit the other account.*

D. *Received a $50 fee for services*

Cash	Income From Fees
50	50

The two accounts affected are Cash and Income From Fees. Did we receive money or did we pay out money? We received money, so we use Simplified Rule 2, *Debit Cash and credit the other account.*

E. *Paid $75 on account*

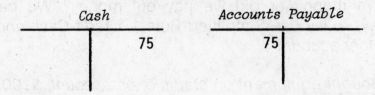

The two accounts affected are Cash and Accounts Payable. Did we receive money or did we pay out money? We paid out money, so we use Simplified Rule 1, *Credit Cash and debit the other account.*

The above graphically illustrates how we use the Three Simplified Rules. Whenever we see the word *paid,* we simply credit Cash and debit the other account. Whenever we see the words *received money* in a transaction, we simply debit Cash and credit the other account. Whenever the transaction is about buying equipment on account, we simply debit Equipment and credit Accounts Payable.

Since we learn by doing, you are going to get your pencil out and do your first homework assignment.

HOMEWORK ASSIGNMENT NO. 1

Use the Three Simplified Rules. Follow these three steps: 1. Read the transaction. 2. Decide which of the Three Simplified Rules applies to the transaction. 3. Make the proper debit and credit entries in the two accounts shown just to the right of the transaction.

Sample Transaction

Paid rent, $900

Now, record the following transactions, following the three steps listed above. It is suggested you use a pencil to make your entries.

A. Bought equipment for cash, $300

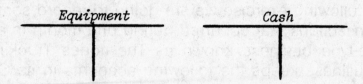

B. Received a $60 fee for services

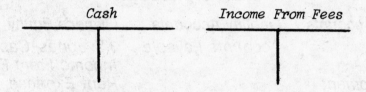

C. Paid $85 on account

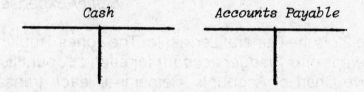

D. Bought equipment on account, $200

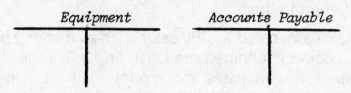

E. Paid $50 for advertising

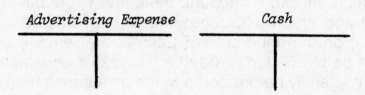

NOTE—Answers to homework start on page 162.

APPLICATION OF PRINCIPLES

In the following exercise we are going to record some typical transactions that occurred during one month in a small service-type business known as The Jones Trucking Co. This business keeps the following accounts in its General Ledger:

Chart of Accounts

Asset Accounts	Liability Accounts	Owner's Equity
Cash	Accounts Payable	J.S. Jones, Capital
Office		Income From Fees
Equipment		Rent Expense
Office Supplies		Telephone Expense
		Truck Expense
		Salary Expense

On page 22 is the General Ledger for The Jones Trucking Co. Note there is *one T ledger account* for each account listed in the above Chart of Accounts. Remember, each transaction will affect two of these accounts, and we will debit one and credit the other. We will use the Three Simplified Rules, so keep referring to them.

A. J.S. Jones invested $5,000 cash in a new trucking business
The two accounts affected are Cash and J.S. Jones, Capital. Since Mr. Jones invested the money in the business, the business is *receiving the money.* This means we use Rule 2, which says whenever we receive money, always debit Cash and credit the other account; therefore, we debit Cash for $5,000 and credit J.S. Jones, Capital, for $5,000. Look at entry (A) on the debit side of Cash and at entry (A) on the credit side of J.S. Jones, Capital. (Read this once again and study it carefully before going to the next transaction.)

B. Paid rent for the month, $600
The two accounts affected are Cash and Rent Expense. Since we paid out money, we use Rule 1, which says whenever we pay out money, always credit Cash and debit the other account; therefore, we credit Cash for $600 and debit Rent Expense for $600. On page 22 look at entry (B) on the

credit side of Cash and at entry (B) on the debit side of Rent Expense.

C. Purchased office equipment for cash, $500

The two accounts affected are Cash and Office Equipment. Since we are paying out money, we again use Rule 1: Credit Cash for $500 and debit Office Equipment for $500. Look at entry (C) on the credit side of Cash and at entry (C) on the debit side of Office Equipment.

D. Received $50 income for services

The two accounts affected are Cash and Income From Fees. Since we received money, we use Rule 2, which says whenever we receive money, always debit Cash and credit the other account; therefore, we debit Cash for $50 and credit Income From Fees for $50. Look at entry (D) on the debit side of Cash and at entry (D) on the credit side of Income From Fees.

E. Paid telephone bill, $38

The two accounts affected are Cash and Telephone Expense. Again we paid out money, so again we use Rule 1: Credit Cash for $38 and debit Telephone Expense for $38. Look at entry (E) on the credit side of Cash and at entry (E) on the debit side of Telephone Expense.

F. Purchased office equipment on account, $100

The two accounts affected are Office Equipment and Accounts Payable. This transaction follows Rule 3; therefore, we debit Office Equipment and credit Accounts Payable. Look at entry (F) on the debit side of Office Equipment and at entry (F) on the credit side of Accounts Payable.

G. Received $75 income for services

The two accounts affected are Cash and Income From Fees. Since we received money, we use Rule 2, which says whenever we receive money, always debit Cash and credit the other account; therefore, we debit Cash for $75 and credit Income From Fees for $75. Look at entry (G) on the debit side of Cash and at entry (G) on the credit side of Income From Fees.

The Jones Trucking Co. - General Ledger

Cash

(A)	5000	(B)	600
(D)	50	(C)	500
(G)	75	(E)	38
		(H)	85
		(I)	5
		(K)	900
		(L)	100

Office Equipment

(C)	500
(F)	100
(J)	150

Office Supplies

(I)	5

Accounts Payable

(L)	100	(F)	100
		(J)	150

J. S. Jones, Capital

		(A)	5000

Income From Fees

		(D)	50
		(G)	75

Rent Expense

(B)	600

Telephone Expense

(E)	38

Truck Expense

(H)	85

Salary Expense

(K)	900

H. Paid $85 for repairs on delivery truck

The two accounts affected are Cash and Truck Expense. Since we paid out money, we use Rule 1; therefore, we credit Cash for $85 and debit Truck Expense for $85. Look at entry (H) on the credit side of Cash and at entry (H) on the debit side of Truck Expense.

I. Purchased office supplies for cash, $5

The two accounts affected are Cash and Office Supplies. Since we paid out money, we use Rule 1; therefore, we credit Cash for $5 and debit Office Supplies for $5. Look at entry (I) on the credit side of Cash and at entry (I) on the debit side of Office Supplies.

J. Purchased office equipment on account, $150

The two accounts affected are Office Equipment and Accounts Payable. This transaction follows Rule 3; therefore, we debit Office Equipment and credit Accounts Payable. Look at entry (J) on the debit side of Office Equipment and at entry (J) on the credit side of Accounts Payable.

K. Paid salaries for month, $900

The two accounts affected are Cash and Salary Expense. Since we paid out money, we use Rule 1; therefore, we credit Cash for $900 and debit Salary Expense for $900. Look at entry (K) on the credit side of Cash and at entry (K) on the debit side of Salary Expense.

L. Paid $100 in full of account for the equipment purchased in transaction (F).

The two accounts affected are Cash and Accounts Payable. Since we paid out money, we use Rule 1; therefore, we credit Cash for $100 and debit Accounts Payable for $100. Look at entry (L) on the credit side of Cash and at entry (L) on the debit side of Accounts Payable. (Note when we make a payment *on account,* or *in full of account,* the other account affected besides Cash is always Accounts Payable.)

The foregoing transactions illustrate, with detailed descriptions, exactly how to apply the Three Simplified Rules. Study these twelve transactions carefully several times; then get your pencil out and do the following assignment.

HOMEWORK ASSIGNMENT NO. 2

Record these transactions in the ledger accounts that follow. Use the Three Simplified Rules. Use the following procedure exactly: 1. Read the transaction. 2. Decide which two accounts are affected by the transaction. 3. If you are paying out money, use Rule 1. 4. If you are receiving money, use Rule 2. 5. If you are purchasing equipment on account, use Rule 3.

When you can record these transactions correctly, you are making excellent progress in learning basic bookkeeping. Keep up the good work!

A. Paid rent for the month, $500
B. Purchased office equipment for cash, $400
C. Received $60 income for services
D. Paid telephone bill, $35
E. Purchased office equipment on account, $125
F. Received $80 income for services
G. Purchased office equipment on account, $175
H. Paid electric bill, $38
I. Paid salaries for month, $800
J. Paid $100 on account

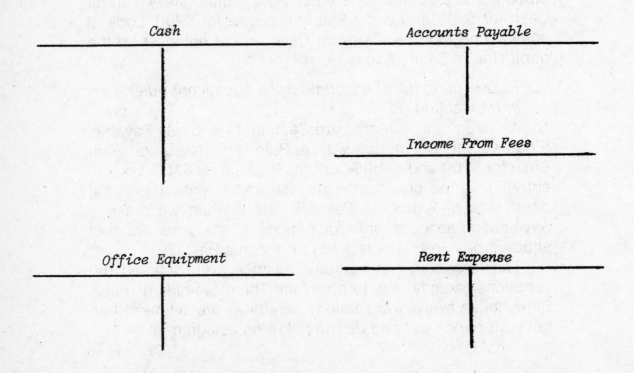

Telephone Expense

Salary Expense

Electric Expense

LESSON THREE

The
General Journal

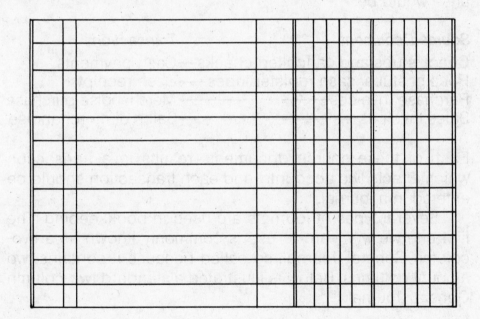

At the outset we stated that bookkeepers and accountants keep records in a *set of books.* These books consist principally of journals and ledgers. Up to this point, you have learned how to record transactions directly in the T ledger accounts. In actual practice, all transactions should be recorded first of all in some type of *journal* and then periodically the figures are posted or transferred from the journal to the individual ledger accounts. For this reason, the journal is called *the book of original entry.*

SOURCE DOCUMENTS

Each transaction to be entered in the journal originates from some written or printed form called a *source document.* Examples of source documents from which transactions arise would be:

Source Document	*Transactions*
Check stubs and cancelled checks→	Cash payments
Receipt stubs, cash register tapes—	Cash receipts
Purchase invoices	Merchandise purchase
Sales invoices	Sales of merchandise

Each of these source documents results in a transaction which affects two accounts, and each transaction should be entered in a journal.

Several types of journals are used in bookkeeping. The first one we will learn to use is commonly known as a two-column General Journal, so called because it contains two amount columns. Below is illustrated a standard two-column General Journal.

Date	Description	P.F.	Debit	Credit

Note that the first column at the left is the date column; then a description column; then the P.R. or posting reference column; and then the two amount columns, the first one being the debit column and the second one being the credit column. In recording a transaction in the General Journal we still use the Three Simplified Rules.

1. When we pay out money, always credit Cash and debit the other account.
2. When we receive money, always debit Cash and credit the other account.
3. When we buy equipment on account, always debit Equipment and credit Accounts Payable.

Example *Jan. 2. Paid rent for the month, $800*
This transaction affects Rent Expense and Cash. Since we paid out money, we credit Cash and debit the other account. This would be recorded in the General Journal as follows:

Date	Description	P.F.	Debit	Credit
Jan 2	RENT EXPENSE		800 —	
	CASH			800 —
	PAID JAN. RENT			

As stated above, we debit Rent Expense and credit Cash. Notice it requires three lines to enter a transaction in the General Journal. The only new rule is this: *In the General Journal, whichever account should be debited is always entered on the first line; whichever account should be credited is entered on the second line.* In this transaction we paid out money, therefore we credited Cash and debited Rent Expense. Since Rent Expense is the account being debited, notice it is written on the first line, and we enter $800 in the debit column. On the second line we write the name of the account to be credited, Cash, and enter $800 in the credit column. On the third line we always write a *brief explanation.* "Paid Jan. rent" was sufficient.

Example *Jan. 3—Purchased office equipment for cash, $300*

JAN 3	OFFICE EQUIPMENT	300 -	
	CASH		300 -
	BOUGHT NEW DESK		

This transaction affects Office Equipment and Cash. Since we paid out money, we again use Simplified Rule 1: Credit Cash and debit the other account. Since Office Equipment should be debited, we write it on the first line and enter $300 in the debit column. On the second line we write Cash, the account being credited, and enter $300 in the credit column. The brief explanation is entered on the third line. Note, also, that on the second line, when we write the name of the account to be credited, it is customary to indent it four or five spaces to the right.

Example *Jan. 7—Received $50 income for services rendered*

Indent ———

JAN 7	CASH	50 -	
	→ INCOME FROM FEES		50 -
	FEE FOR SERVICES		

This transaction affects Cash and Income From Fees. Since we are receiving money, we use Simplified Rule 2: Debit Cash and credit the other account. Since Cash is the account being debited, we write it on the first line and enter $50 in the debit column. On the second line we indent five spaces and write the name of the account being credited, Income From Fees, and enter $50 in the credit column. The brief explanation is entered on the third line.

PRACTICAL PROBLEM

The following are some typical transactions for an entire month for the George Van Moving Co. These transactions have been entered in the General Journal on page 33. Read each transaction carefully and note how it was entered in the General Journal.

Asset Accounts	Liability Accounts	Owner's Equity
Cash	Accounts Payable	George Van, Capital
Office		Income From Fees
Equipment		Rent Expense
		Telephone Expense
		Truck Expense

May 1. The owner, George Van, invested $5,000 cash in a new business

This transaction affects Cash and George Van, Capital. Since the business is receiving the money invested in it, we use Rule 2: Debit Cash and credit the other account. Since Cash is being debited, we write it first and enter $5,000 in the debit column. On the second line we indent and write the name of the account being credited, George Van, Capital, and enter $5,000 in the credit column. The brief explanation is written on the third line.

May 2. Paid rent for the month, $600

The two accounts affected are Cash and Rent Expense. Since we are paying out money we use Rule 1, Credit Cash and debit the other account. As Rent Expense is being debited, we write it first and enter $600 in the debit column. On the second line we indent and write the name of the account being credited, Cash, and enter $600 in the credit column. The explanation is entered on the next line.

May 6. Bought office equipment for cash, $300

The two accounts affected are Office Equipment and Cash. Since we are paying out money, we use Rule 1: Credit Cash and debit the other account. As Office Equipment is being debited, we write it first and enter $300 in the debit column.

On the second line we write the name of the account being credited, Cash, and enter $300 in the credit column.

May 10. Received $500 income for services
The two accounts affected are Cash and Income From Fees. Since we are receiving money, we use Rule 2: Debit Cash and credit the other account. Since Cash is being debited, we write it first and enter $500 in the debit column. On the second line we write the name of the account being credited, Income From Fees, and enter $500 in the credit column.

May 12. Paid telephone bill, $38
The two accounts affected are Cash and Telephone Expense. Since we are paying out money, we use Rule 1: Credit Cash and debit the other account. As Telephone Expense is being debited, we write it first and enter $38 in the debit column. On the second line we write the name of the account being credited, Cash, and enter $38 in the credit column.

May 14. Bought office equipment on account, $430
The two accounts affected are Office Equipment and Accounts Payable. This transaction follows Simplified Rule 3, so we debit Office Equipment and credit Accounts Payable.

May 17. Received $500 income for services
The two accounts affected are Cash and Income From Fees. Since we are receiving money, we use Rule 2: Debit Cash and credit the other account. Since Cash is being debited, we write it first and enter $500 in the debit column. On the second line we write the name of the account being credited, Income From Fees, and enter $500 in the credit column.

May 20. Paid for repairs on truck, $65
The two accounts affected are Cash and Truck Expense. Since we are paying out money, we use Rule 1: Credit Cash and debit the other account. As Truck Expense is being debited, we write it first and enter $65 in the debit column. On the second line we write the name of the account being credited, Cash, and enter $65 in the credit column.

General Journal

Date		Description	P.F.	Debit	Credit
May	1	Cash		5000 -	
		Geo. Van, Capital			5000 -
		Investment in business			
	2	Rent Expense		600 -	
		Cash			600 -
		Paid May rent			
	6	Office Equipment		300 -	
		Cash			300 -
		Bought equipment			
	10	Cash		500 -	
		Income From Fees			500 -
		Received for services			
	12	Telephone Expense		38 -	
		Cash			38 -
		May tel. bill			
	14	Office Equipment		430 -	
		Accounts Payable			430 -
		Bought on account			
	17	Cash		500 -	
		Income From Fees			500 -
	20	Truck Expense		65 -	
		Cash			65 -
		Repairs on truck			
	21	Accounts Payable		100 -	
		Cash			100 -
		Paid on account			

May 21. Paid $100 on account

The two accounts affected are Cash and Accounts Payable. Since we are paying out money, we use Rule 1: Credit Cash and debit the other account. As Accounts Payable is being debited, we write it first and enter $100 in the debit column. On the second line we write the name of the account being credited, Cash, and enter $100 in the credit column.

HOMEWORK ASSIGNMENT NO. 3

Now, you are to use a pencil and do the following homework assignment. Follow this procedure: 1. Read the transaction. 2. Decide which two accounts are affected. 3. Decide which account should be debited and which one should be credited. (Remember, the *debit* account should always be entered first.) 4. Make the proper entry in the General Journal on three lines, using the Three Simplified Rules. Each transaction will affect two of the following accounts:

Chart of Accounts

Cash	James Jones, Capital	Telephone
Office Equipment	Income From Fees	Expense
Accounts Payable	Rent Expense	Truck Expense

Jan 2. The owner, James Jones, invested $7,000 cash in a new business

Jan. 3. Paid rent for the month, $500

Jan. 6. Purchased a new desk for cash, $200

Jan. 10. Received $600 income for services

Jan. 12. Paid telephone bill, $41

Jan. 14. Purchased a desk on account, $560

Jan. 17. Received $400 income for services

Jan. 20. Paid for repairs on truck, $75

Jan. 21. Paid $260 on account

General Journal

Date	Description	P.F.	Debit	Credit

POSTING

As we have seen, the purpose of the General Journal is to provide a chronological record of the transactions completed during the month. From time to time, the amounts entered in the journal should be *posted* or transferred from the journal to the individual T ledger accounts. This posting may be done daily, at frequent intervals during the month, or at the end of the month. When a transaction is entered in the journal, one account is debited on the first line and the other account is credited on the next line. *Posting* consists of transferring a figure from the debit column of the journal to the debit side of the proper account in the ledger, then transferring the same figure from the credit side of the journal to the credit side of the proper account in the ledger.

(In actual practice, the journal entries are together in one book called the General Journal. The T ledger accounts are together in another bound book called the General Ledger. The General Journal and the General Ledger would both be open in front of the bookkeeper as he proceeded to post each figure from the journal to the ledger. In the illustrations to follow we show the journal entry, then we show the two ledger accounts immediately below the journal entry in order to help you understand the proper procedure for posting. However, remember the actual procedure would be as just explained.)

The following entry appeared in the George Van Moving Co. General Journal on page 33.

MAY 1	CASH	5 000 —		
	GEO. VAN, CAP.		5 000 —	
	INITIAL INVESTMENT			

In this transaction we debited Cash for $5,000 and credited George Van, Capital, for $5,000. This means that when posting, we should post the first $5,000 to the debit side of the Cash account in the ledger, using the date of May 1; we then post the other $5,000 to the credit side of the George Van,

Capital, account in the ledger, using the date of May 1. The following illustrates exactly how this is done.

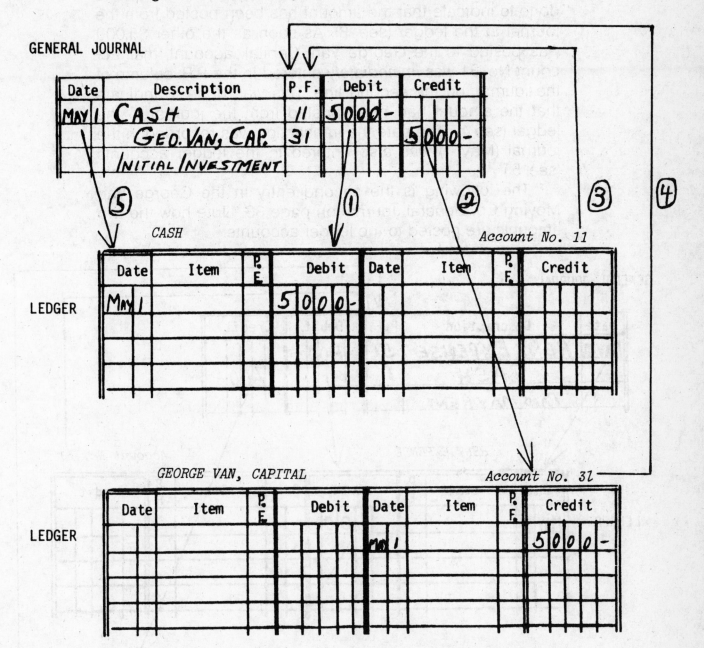

GENERAL JOURNAL

Date	Description	P.F.	Debit	Credit
MAY 1	CASH	11	5000-	
	GEO. VAN, CAP.	31		5000-
	INITIAL INVESTMENT			

LEDGER

CASH   Account No. 11

Date	Item	P.F.	Debit	Date	Item	P.F.	Credit
MAY 1			5000-				

LEDGER

GEORGE VAN, CAPITAL   Account No. 31

Date	Item	P.F.	Debit	Date	Item	P.F.	Credit
				MAY 1			5000-

It has often been said that when posting we "do just what the journal says." The journal above says to debit Cash for $5,000; therefore, we post the first $5,000 to the debit side of the Cash account in the ledger (see 1). Then the journal says George Van, Capital, credit $5,000; therefore, we post the other $5,000 to the credit side of George Van, Capital in the ledger (see 2). As soon as the first $5,000 was posted to the

Cash account in the ledger, we *immediately* enter the Cash account No. 11 in the P.R. column of the journal. This is done to indicate that the amount has been posted from the journal to the ledger (see 3). As soon as the other $5,000 was posted to the George Van, Capital, account, *that* account No. 31 was *immediately* entered in the P.R. column of the journal, on the second line. This was done to indicate that the amount had been posted from the journal to the ledger (see 4). The date the transaction was recorded in the journal (May 1) was also entered in the ledger accounts (see 5).

The following is the second entry in the George Van Moving Co. General Journal on page 33. Note how the two amounts are posted to the ledger accounts.

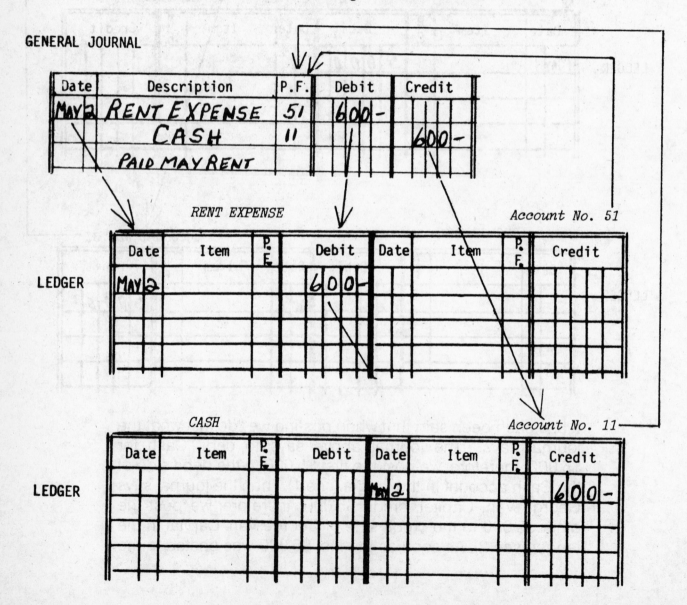

The following is the third entry in the George Van Moving Co.
General Journal on page 33. Note how the two amounts are
posted to the ledger accounts.

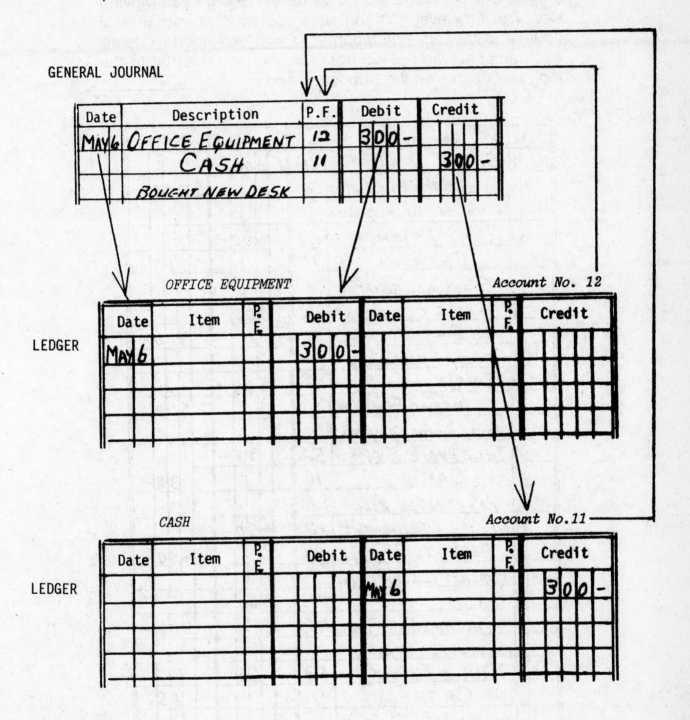

GENERAL JOURNAL

Date	Description	P.F.	Debit	Credit
MAY 6	OFFICE EQUIPMENT	12	300 —	
	CASH	11		300 —
	BOUGHT NEW DESK			

OFFICE EQUIPMENT   Account No. 12

LEDGER

Date	Item	P.F.	Debit	Date	Item	P.F.	Credit
MAY 6			300 —				

CASH   Account No. 11

LEDGER

Date	Item	P.F.	Debit	Date	Item	P.F.	Credit
				MAY 6			300 —

POSTING THE COMPLETE GENERAL JOURNAL

On the following pages you will find the entire General Journal and the ledger accounts for the George Van Moving Co. Note how every amount was posted from the General Journal to the ledger accounts. As just explained in detail, each amount was posted from this General Journal to the ledger accounts on the opposite page. ⟶

Date	Description	P.F.	Debit	Credit
MAY 1	CASH	11	5000 —	
	GEORGE VAN, CAP.	31		5000 —
	INITIAL INVESTMENT			
2	RENT EXPENSE	51	600 —	
	CASH	11		600 —
	PAID MAY RENT			
6	OFFICE EQUIPMENT	12	300 —	
	CASH	11		300 —
	BOUGHT NEW DESK			
10	CASH	11	500 —	
	INCOME FROM FEES	41		500 —
	RECEIVED FOR SERVICES			
12	TELEPHONE EXP.	52	38 —	
	CASH	11		38 —
	PAID MAY TEL. BILL			
14	OFFICE EQUIPMENT	12	430 —	
	ACCOUNTS PAYABLE	21		430 —
	PURCH. FILE ON ACCOUNT			
17	CASH	11	500 —	
	INCOME FROM FEES	41		500 —
	RECEIVED FOR SERVICES			
20	TRUCK EXPENSE	53	65 —	
	CASH	11		65 —
	PD. FOR REPAIRS ON TRUCK			
21	ACCOUNTS PAYABLE	21	100 —	
	CASH	11		100 —
	PAID ON ACCOUNT			

GEORGE VAN MOVING CO. - GENERAL LEDGER

Cash			No. 11
MAY 1	5000-	MAY 2	600-
10	500-	6	300-
17	500-	12	38-
		20	65-
		21	100-

Income From Fees			No. 41
		MAY 10	500-
		17	500-

Office Equipment		No. 12
MAY 6	300-	
14	430-	

Rent Expense		No. 51
MAY 2	600-	

Accounts Payable			No. 21
MAY 21	100-	MAY 14	430-

Telephone Expense		No. 52
MAY 12	38-	

George Van, Capital			No. 31
		MAY 1	5000-

Truck Expense		No. 53
MAY 20	65-	

HOMEWORK ASSIGNMENT NO. 4

Post every amount from this journal to the ledger accounts on the following page. Follow the procedure outlined on the preceding pages.

Date	Description	P.F.	Debit	Credit
Jan 1	CASH		6000 -	
	RAY BROWN, CAP.			6000 -
	INITIAL INVESTMENT			
2	RENT EXPENSE		700 -	
	CASH			700 -
6	OFFICE EQUIPMENT		300 -	
	CASH			300 -
	PURCH. NEW EQUIPMENT			
9	CASH		900 -	
	INCOME FROM FEES			900 -
	RECEIVED FOR SERVICES			
11	TELEPHONE EXP.		73 -	
	CASH			73 -
	PAID JAN. TEL. BILL			
16	OFFICE EQUIPMENT		550 -	
	ACCOUNTS PAYABLE			550 -
	PURCH EQUIP. ON ACCOUNT			
19	CASH		900 -	
	INCOME FROM FEES			900 -
	RECEIVED FOR SERVICES			
21	TRUCK EXPENSE		41 -	
	CASH			41 -
	REPAIRS ON TRUCK			
26	ACCOUNTS PAYABLE		250 -	
	CASH			250 -
	PAID ON ACCOUNT			

RAY BROWN CO. — GENERAL LEDGER

Cash   No. 11   Income From Fees   No. 41

Office Equipment   No. 12   Rent Expense   No. 51

Accounts Payable   No. 21   Telephone Expense   No. 52

Ray Brown, Capital   No. 31   Truck Expense   No. 53

THE TRIAL BALANCE

At the end of each month, after all amounts have been posted from the journal to the ledger accounts, it is customary to take a Trial Balance. The purpose of the Trial Balance is to prove that the ledger is "in balance." It will also be used later in preparing the various financial statements. Since we made a debit and a credit of the same amount for each transaction, it follows that the sum of all the debit entries should equal the sum of all the credit entries. However, instead of totaling all the debit and credit entries, we list all the account *balances* on the Trial Balance and total these *balances*. The proper procedure for finding the *balance* of a ledger account is as follows:

Footing the Ledger Accounts

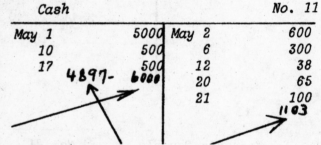

When the account has figures on both sides, total the debit side and write the total ($6,000) in *small* pencil figures directly under the last debit entry. Total the credit side and write the total ($1,103) in small pencil figures directly under the last credit entry. These totals are called *footings*. Subtract the smaller total from the larger ($6,000 minus $1,103) and write the difference ($4,897) on the larger side, just to the left of the total. The difference between the two footings is called the *balance* of the account. The balance is always written on the side with the larger total, in this case the debit side. We now say the Cash account has *a debit balance* of $4,897, and this amount will be entered on the debit side of the Trial Balance.

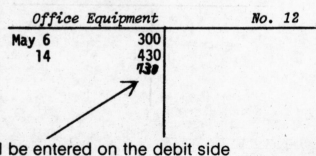

In the Office Equipment account we foot the debit side ($730), and since there is nothing on the credit side to be subtracted, we say Office Equipment has a debit balance of $730. This amount will be entered on the debit side of the Trial Balance.

In the Accounts Payable account there is nothing to be added on either the debit or credit side. However, we still subtract one side from the other ($430 minus $100) and write the difference ($330) on the larger side, in this case the credit side. We say Accounts Payable has a credit balance of $330, and this amount will be entered on the credit side of the Trial Balance.

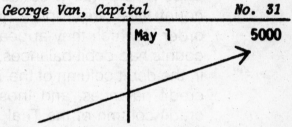

Accounts Payable			No. 21
May 21	100	May 14	330 430

In the George Van, Capital, account, since there is only one entry, there is nothing to add or subtract. Without doing anything to the account, we say it has a credit balance of $5,000, and this is the amount that will be entered on the credit side of the Trial Balance.

George Van, Capital		No. 31
	May 1	5000

George Van Moving Co.
Trial Balance
May 31

	Dr.	Cr.
Cash	4 8 9 7 0 0	
Office Equipment	7 3 0 0 0	
Accounts Payable		3 3 0 0 0
George Van, Capital		5 0 0 0 0 0
Income From Fees		1 0 0 0 0 0
Rent Expense	6 0 0 0 0	
Telephone Expense	3 8 0 0	
Truck Expense	6 5 0 0	
	6 3 3 0 0 0	6 3 3 0 0 0

This is the Trial Balance taken from the George Van Moving Co. ledger accounts on page 47. Note that each account that contains amounts on both sides has been footed and the balance has been entered on the larger side, exactly as explained on the preceding two pages. Note that those accounts that contain only *one* entry do not need to be footed since that single entry is also the balance of the account.

The Trial Balance is taken on a sheet of General Journal paper, or on a form that is ruled similar to General Journal paper. Note that it contains a three-line heading. The account titles are copied on the Trial Balance in the same order in which they appear in the ledger. Note that five accounts had debit balances, and those balances were entered in the debit column of the Trial Balance. Three accounts had credit balances, and those balances were entered in the credit column of the Trial Balance. When the Trial Balance was footed, it was found that the debit and credit columns had the same total, $6,330. This means that the ledger accounts are "in balance," indicating that we have recorded a debit for every credit in the journal and that we have correctly posted all amounts from the journal to the ledger.

If the debit and credit columns of the Trial Balance do not equal one another, we know that we have probably made some common type of error. In that case, we should check back until we find the error, so that the books will be in balance.

General Ledger

Cash				No. 11
May 1	5000	May 2		600
10	500	6		300
17	4897- 6600 500	12		38
		20		65
		21		100
				1103

Income From Fees		No. 41
	May 10	500
	17	500
		1000

Office Equipment		No. 12
May 6	300	
14	430	
	730	

Rent Expense		No. 51
May 2	600	

Accounts Payable			No. 21
May 21	100	May 14	330- 430

Telephone Expense		No. 52
May 12	38	

George Van, Capital		No. 31
	May 1	5000

Truck Expense		No. 53
May 20	65	

Bill Barnes, Architect
Trial Balance
January 31

		Debit		Credit

HOMEWORK ASSIGNMENT NO. 5 For this homework assignment you need to use a pencil and foot the ledger accounts for Bill Barnes, Architect, on page 49 and then take a Trial Balance above. In the Cash account you should total the debit side, total the credit side, subtract one total from the other and write the balance on the larger side (see page 44). In the Office Equipment account, total the two debits—that total is also the balance. In the Accounts Payable account, subtract one side from the other and write the balance on the larger side (see page 45). As there is only one amount in the Bill Barnes, Capital account, that amount is also the balance of the account. Total the two credit entries in Income From Fees—and that total is also the balance. The other three accounts each contain one entry, so those entries are the balances of those accounts.

Copy the names of all the accounts in the above Trial Balance and also copy the balance for each account. Five of the accounts should have debit balances which should be entered in the debit column of the Trial Balance; three of the accounts should have credit balances which should be entered in the credit column.

Total the two columns of the Trial Balance; those totals should be the same.

General Ledger
Bill Barnes, Architect

Cash				No. 11
Jan 1	3000	Jan 2	500	
10	300	6	400	
17	300	12	52	
		20	73	
		21	100	

Income From Fees		No. 41
	Jan 10	300
	17	300

Office Equipment		No. 12
Jan 6	400	
14	350	

Rent Expense		No. 51
Jan 2	500	

Accounts Payable			No. 21
Jan 21	100	Jan 14	350

Telephone Expense		No. 52
Jan 12	52	

Bill Barnes, Capital		No. 31
	Jan 1	3000

Electric Expense		No. 53
Jan 20	73	

THE BOOKKEEPING CYCLE

We have now learned how to complete the first four steps of what is known as the Bookkeeping Cycle. These steps consist of the following:

1. Journalizing the day-to-day transactions in the General Journal.
2. Posting from the journal to the ledger accounts.
3. Footing the ledger accounts.
4. Taking a Trial Balance.

As a means of reviewing and reinforcing the learning process, you will next do a complete problem, utilizing all four steps of the Bookkeeping Cycle. It is recommended that this exercise be done with a pencil.

HOMEWORK ASSIGNMENT NO. 6

Record each transaction below in the General Journal. Analyze each transaction in the following manner: 1. Read the transaction. 2. Look at the Chart of Accounts and decide which two accounts are affected. 3. Decide which of the Three Simplified Rules applies. 4. Do what the rule says, remembering that the account to be debited is entered first; the account to be credited is entered on the second line; a brief explanation is written on the third line.

Chart of Accounts

Cash	Dry Cleaning Income
Dry Cleaning Equipment	Rent Expense
Accounts Payable	Telephone Expense
Joe Cross, Capital	Advertising Expense

May 1. The owner invested $7,000 cash in Joe Cross Cleaners
May 2. Paid rent for May, $600
May 5. Received $650 for dry cleaning services
May 8. Purchased cleaning machinery on credit, $1,200
May 12. Paid April telephone bill, $42
May 18. Received $850 for dry cleaning services
May 20. Paid Daily Post $85 for advertising
May 22. Purchased more equipment on credit, $600
May 28. Paid $300 on account

Joe Cross Cleaners
General Journal

Date		Description	P.F.	Debit	Credit	

Post every figure from the General Journal to the ledger accounts below. Use the same posting procedure you followed on pages 42 and 43. As soon as a figure is posted from the journal to the ledger, be sure to enter the account number in the Posting Reference (P.R.) column of the journal.

Joe Cross Cleaners - General Ledger

Cash   No. 11

Dry Cleaning Income   No. 41

Dry Cleaning Equipment   No. 12

Rent Expense   No. 51

Accounts Payable   No. 21

Telephone Expense   No. 52

Joe Cross, Capital   No. 31

Advertising Expense   No. 53

When you have completed the posting from the journal to the ledger, foot all the ledger accounts when necessary, write the balance on the larger side of the account. Take a Trial Balance on the form below. In footing the accounts and taking the Trial Balance, use the same procedure you followed on pages 48 and 49.

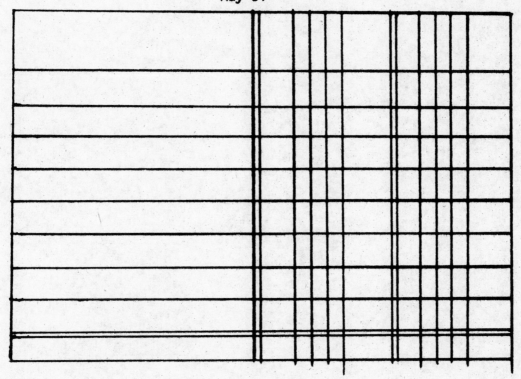

Joe Cross Cleaners
Trial Balance
May 31

Note: As previously noted, all four elements of the Bookkeeping Cycle are incorporated in this problem. When you are able to complete this problem correctly and get the Trial Balance, you are making real progress!

LESSON FOUR

The Four-Column Cash Journal

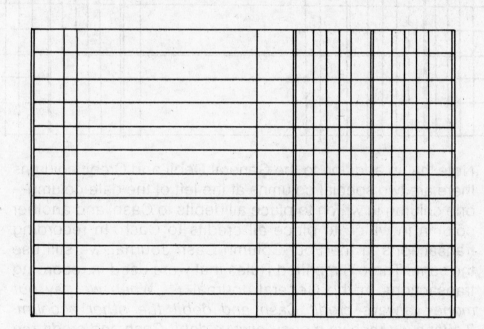

We have learned that each transaction affects two accounts. You have probably noted that in a large number of transactions one of the two accounts affected is the Cash account. The reason is that in the average personal service type of business enterprise the majority of the transactions involve either the receipt of money or the paying out of money. It has, therefore, often been found to be advantageous to use a special *Four-Column Cash Journal* in place of the two-column General Journal. As we shall see, one of the features of a Four-Column Cash Journal is that it considerably reduces the many time-consuming debit and credit postings to the Cash account in the ledger. Here is an illustration of a typical Four-Column Cash Journal.

CASH		Date	Description	P R	GENERAL	
Debit	Credit				Debit	Credit

Note that in addition to the General Debit and Credit columns there are two special columns at the left of the date column— one column in which to place all debits to Cash, and another column in which to place all credits to Cash. In recording transactions in the Four-Column Cash Journal, we still use the same Three Simplified Rules that were used in recording transactions in the General Journal. *(1. When we pay out money, always credit Cash and debit the other account. 2. When we receive money, always debit Cash and credit the other account. 3. When we buy equipment on account, always debit Equipment and credit Accounts Payable.)*

Most transactions can be recorded on one line in the Cash Journal, instead of using three lines as we did in the General Journal. Each transaction should first be analyzed in the same manner as previously illustrated.

Example *June 1. Paid rent for the month, $600.* What two accounts are affected? Cash and Rent Expense. Which rule applies? Since we are paying out money, we use Rule 1: Credit Cash and debit the other account. The transaction would be entered in the two-column General Journal in this manner:

Jun	1	Rent Expense			6 0 0 -		
		Cash				6 0 0 -	
		Paid June rent					

Here is the same transaction entered in the Four-Column Cash Journal.

CASH				P	GENERAL	
Debit	Credit	Date	Description	R	Debit	Credit
	6 0 0 -	Jun 1	Rent Expense		6 0 0 -	

Note we credit Cash and debit Rent Expense. The *way* we credit Cash is to simply enter $600 in the Cash Credit column, which is the second column on the left. Just writing $600 in that column indicates we are crediting Cash. Next, we debit Rent Expense. This is done by writing Rent Expense in the Description column and entering $600 in the General Debit column. Note that all this is accomplished on one line in the Cash Journal. The brief explanation which was written on the third line in the General Journal is usually omitted in the Cash Journal. This is customary accounting practice since in most instances, the entries explain themselves.

Example *June 5. Received from Jones Co. $50 for services rendered.* What two accounts are affected? Cash and Income From Fees. Which rule applies? Since we are receiving money, we use Rule 2: Debit Cash and credit the other account. Here it is entered in the Two-Column Journal.

Jun 5	Cash		50 –	
	Income From Fees			50 –
	Rec'd. from Jones Co.			

Here is the same transaction entered in the Four-Column Cash Journal.

CASH		Date	Description	P R	GENERAL	
Debit	Credit				Debit	Credit
50 –		Jun 5	Income From Fees			50 –

Note we debit Cash and credit Income From Fees. The *way* we debit Cash is to simply enter $50 in the Cash Debit column, which is the first column on the left. Just writing $50 in that column indicates we are debiting Cash. Next, we credit Income From Fees. This is done by writing Income From Fees in the Description column and entering $50 in the General Credit column. Note the transaction is entered on one line.

Example *June 7. Bought office equipment on account, $300.* What two accounts are affected? Office Equipment and Accounts Payable. Which rule applies? Rule 3 applies, so we debit Office Equipment and credit Accounts Payable. Here it is entered in the General Journal.

Jun	7	Office Equipment		3 0 0 -		
		Accounts Payable			3 0 0 -	
		Purch. on account				

Here is the same transaction entered in the Four-Column Cash Journal.

CASH					P R	GENERAL	
Debit	Credit	Date	Description			Debit	Credit
		Jun 7	Office Equipment			3 0 0 -	
			Accounts Payable				3 0 0 -

Note we debit Office Equipment and credit Accounts Payable. Since the Cash account was not affected by this transaction, we did not use either of the two Cash columns. Instead, the transaction is entered in the General Debit and Credit columns, using two lines. Actually, the transaction is entered in the Cash Journal exactly the same way it is entered in the General Journal.

Example *June 9. Paid $100 on account.* What two accounts are affected? Cash and Accounts Payable. Which rule applies? Since we are paying out money, we use Rule 1: Credit Cash and debit the other account. Here is the entry in the General Journal.

Jun	9	Accounts Payable		1 0 0 -		
		Cash			1 0 0 -	
		Paid on account				

Here is the same transaction entered in the Four-Column Cash Journal.

CASH					P	GENERAL	
Debit	Credit	Date	Description		R	Debit	Credit
	1 0 0 –	Jun 9	Accounts Payable			1 0 0 –	

Note we credit Cash and debit Accounts Payable. The way we credit Cash is to enter $100 in the Cash Credit column, which is the second column on the left. Just writing $100 in that column indicates we are crediting Cash. Next, we debit Accounts Payable. This is done by writing Accounts Payable in the Description column and entering $100 in the General Debit column. Note the transaction is entered on one line.

Here are these same transactions entered in one Four-Column Cash Journal. Read each transaction and note how it is entered in the Cash Journal.

June 1. Paid rent for the month, $600
June 5. Received from Jones Co. $50 for services rendered.
June 7. Bought office equipment on account, $300
June 9. Paid $100 on account

CASH				Date	Description	P R	GENERAL		
Debit		Credit					Debit		Credit
		6 0 0 -		Jun 1	Rent Expense		6 0 0 -		
5 0 -				5	Income From Fees				5 0 -
				7	Office Equipment		3 0 0 -		
					Accounts Payable				3 0 0 -
		1 0 0 -		9	Accounts Payable		1 0 0 -		
5 0 -		7 0 0 -					1 0 0 0 -		3 5 0 -

FOOTING AND PROVING THE CASH JOURNAL

At the end of the month the four columns of the Cash Journal should be totaled, or footed, and the totals should be proved. To prove the footings, we add the two Debit columns (Cash Debit and General Debit); this total should equal the sum of the two Credit columns (Cash Credit and General Credit). The following is an illustration of a proof of the above footings.

Cash Debit	50.00	Cash Credit	700.00
General Debit	1000.00	General Credit	350.00
	1050.00		1050.00

Note the sum of the Debit column footings equal the sum of the Credit column footings. If the footings do not prove, then all entries and calculations should be checked until the error is found.

POSTING FROM THE FOUR-COLUMN CASH JOURNAL

Next, we will learn how to post from a Four-Column Cash Journal to the individual ledger accounts. The following is the proper procedure for posting.

| CASH | | | Date | Description | P R | GENERAL | |
Debit	Credit					Debit	Credit
	600-	Jn 1		Rent Expense	51	600-	
50-		5		Income From Fees	41		50-
		7		Office Equipment	12	300-	
				Accounts Payable	21		300-
	100-	9		Accounts Payable	21	100-	
50-	700-					1000-	350-

(1)   (2)

Cash   No. 11

June 30   50- | June 30   700-

Accounts Payable   No. 21

June 9   100- | June 7   300-

Office Equipment   No. 12

June 7   300- |

Income From Fees   No. 41

| June 5   50-

Rent Expense   No. 51

June 1   600- |

First, we post *each* figure from the two General columns to the ledger accounts. This is done *exactly the same way* we posted from a General Journal (see pages 36 to 40). The $600 entry in the General Debit column is posted to the debit side of Rent Expense. The account number for Rent Expense, No. 51, is immediately entered in the P.R. (posting reference) column of the Cash Journal to indicate that the amount has been posted. The $50 entry in the General Credit column is posted to the credit side of Income From Fees. The $300 entry in the General Debit column is posted to the debit side of Office Equipment. The $300 entry in the General Credit column is posted to the credit side of Accounts Payable. The $100 entry in the General Debit column is posted to the debit side of Accounts Payable.

Next we post from the two Cash columns. Since every amount in the first column is a debit to Cash, we post the total of that column. The total, $50, is posted to the debit side of the Cash account in the ledger (see 1). Remember, this is called *summary posting.* Since every amount in the second column is a credit to Cash, we post the total of that column. The total, $700, is posted to the credit side of the Cash account (see 2).

It is evident that being able to post totals from the first two columns of the Cash Journal saves considerable time and effort over what would have been required had the transactions been entered in a General Journal instead of the Four-Column Cash Journal. For example, over the period of a month a small business could easily have ten entries requiring debits to Cash and twenty entries requiring credits to Cash. If entered in a General Journal, these entries would require thirty separate postings to the ledger accounts. These same transactions entered in a Cash Journal would require only *two* postings to the ledger instead of thirty.

You are to record the following transactions in the Four-Column Cash Journal below. Follow the procedures outlined on pages 57 to 60.

HOMEWORK ASSIGNMENT NO. 7

Jan. 1. Paid rent for the month, $700
Jan. 5. Received from James Co. $30 for services
        rendered
Jan. 7. Bought office equipment on account, $400
Jan. 9. Paid $200 on account

CASH			Date	Description	P R	GENERAL	
Debit	Credit					Debit	Credit

After you have finished journalizing the transactions, foot the
four amount columns and prove the footings (see page 61).

Next, you are to post from the Cash Journal to the ledger
accounts below. Follow the procedure outlined on page 63.

Cash   No. 11   Accounts Payable   No. 21

Office Equipment   No. 12   Income From Fees   No. 41

                                            Rent Expense   No. 51

First, post *each amount* from the two General columns of the Cash Journal.

Next, post the *totals* from the two Cash columns.

The last step, of course, which you are not required to do in this problem, would be to foot the ledger accounts and take a Trial Balance.

LESSON FIVE

Accounting
for Merchandise

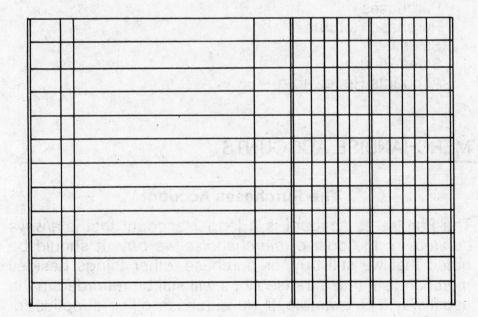

In preceding lessons, we have learned how to record typical transactions for a *personal-service* type of business, such as the George Van Moving Co. and Joe Cross Cleaners. In these two enterprises, money was received as fees for services rendered. In a broad sense, this is referred to as *keeping books on the cash basis.*

Actually, of course, many businesses are not service-oriented but are *retail* and *wholesale* enterprises. In a retail business, money is received because some kind of merchandise is sold. Merchandise is sold either for cash or on credit; and, of course, the stock of merchandise to be sold must first be purchased, either for cash or on credit. In accounting for a retail merchandising business, which we will study next, we will be using the following new ledger accounts, in addition to those previously used:

Purchases
Purchase Returns
Sales
Sales Returns
Accounts Receivable

MERCHANDISE ACCOUNTS

The Purchases Account

The Purchases account is a ledger account that is *always debited* for the cost of *merchandise we buy.* It should be noted that we still buy, or purchase, other things besides merchandise; these transactions will still be recorded in the usual way. For example, if we purchase office supplies for cash, we debit Office Supplies and credit Cash. If we purchase office equipment on account, we debit Office Equipment and credit Accounts Payable. However, when we purchase *merchandise* (our stock in trade) for cash, we debit *Purchases* and credit Cash. Note this transaction follows Simplified Rule 1: When we pay out money, we always credit Cash and debit the other account. Simplified Rule 3 says: When we buy equipment on account, debit Equipment and credit Accounts Payable. Therefore, when we buy *merchandise* on account, we debit Purchases and credit Accounts Payable. In a way, it would seem logical that when we buy merchandise, the account should be called *Merchandise.* However, in accounting, when we buy merchandise, the account is called *Purchases.*

To summarize: When we buy merchandise for cash, debit Purchases and credit Cash; when we buy merchandise on account, debit Purchases and credit Accounts Payable.

In recording purchases of merchandise in a General Journal, the transactions would be recorded as follows:

June 1. Purchased merchandise for cash, $100
June 2. Purchased merchandise on account from Morse Co., $200

Jun 1	Purchases		1 0 0 -			
	Cash				1 0 0 -	
	Bought mdse. for cash					
Jun 2	Purchases		2 0 0 -			
	Accounts Payable				2 0 0 -	
	Bought mdse. from Morse					

THE PURCHASES RETURNS ACCOUNT

Purchases Returns, as the name indicates, is an account in which we record the cost of merchandise returned to a creditor or supplier. The account should always be credited for the cost of merchandise returned. For example, if we returned merchandise purchased for cash, this would affect Cash and Purchases Returns. Since we are receiving money, we follow Simplified Rule 2: Debit Cash and credit Purchases Returns. When we return merchandise purchased on credit, we would debit Accounts payable and credit Purchases Returns. The source document for these transactions is a credit memorandum issued by the creditor. The transactions would be entered in a General Journal as follows:

June 8. Received a $50 refund for merchandise returned
June 9. Received credit for $75 for merchandise returned
to Morse Co.

Jun	8	Cash		5 0	–					
		Purchases Returns					5 0	–		
		Received cash refund								
Jun	9	Accounts Payable		7 5	–					
		Purchases Returns					7 5	–		
		Re'cd. Cr. from Morse								

To summarize: Purchases returns is always credited for the cost of merchandise returned to a supplier. If it was a cash transaction, debit Cash and credit Purchases Returns; if it was a credit transaction, debit Accounts Payable and credit Purchases Returns.

The Purchases Journal

As we have just seen, all transactions arising from a retail merchandising enterprise can be recorded in a two-column General Journal. However, in a business where merchandise purchases occur frequently, most of these purchases are made on account; it has been found that such transactions may be recorded advantageously in a special journal called the *Purchases Journal.*

A commonly used form for a Purchases Journal is illustrated next, with the following transactions recorded in it.

June 1. Received Invoice No. 1 from Watson Co. for mer-
chandise purchased, $200. Terms, net 30 days
June 5. Received Invoice No. 2 from Able Co. for mer-
chandise purchases, $300. Terms, net 30 days

Purchases Journal

Date	Inv.	From Whom Purchased		Amount	
Jun 1	1	Watson Co.		200	-
5	2	Able Co.		300	-

It will be noted that each transaction originated with a *purchase invoice,* which was received from the supplier from whom the merchandise was purchased. The purchase invoice, then, is the source document. The following information was entered on one line of the Purchases Journal for each transaction:

1. Date the purchase invoice was received
2. Number of the invoice
3. From whom purchased
4. Amount of the invoice

POSTING FROM THE PURCHASES JOURNAL

Although each transaction affects two accounts, you will note we do not show a debit and a credit when we enter an invoice in the Purchases Journal. It is not necessary to indicate the two accounts affected, as only one kind of transaction is entered in a Purchases Journal; namely, merchandise purchased on account. Since we have just learned that when we purchase merchandise on account we debit Purchases and credit Accounts Payable, it is understood that these are the two accounts affected by an entry in the Purchases Journal. Therefore, we simply enter each purchase invoice on one line in the Purchases Journal; then at the end of the month we total the journal and post that total to the proper two accounts in the ledger. Note that in the Purchases Journal on the same line with the total, we write:

"Debit Purchases and credit Accounts Payable," and that is exactly the way we post the total. See illustration below.

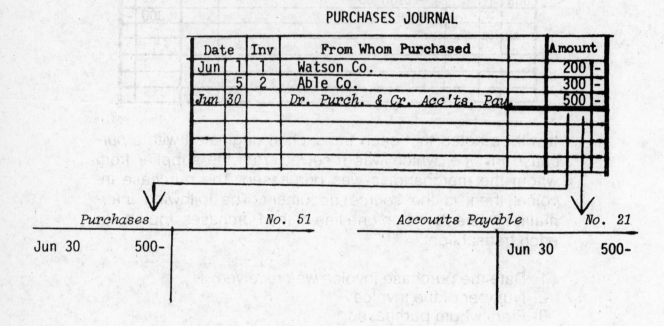

PURCHASES JOURNAL

Date		Inv	From Whom Purchased		Amount	
Jun	1	1	Watson Co.		200	-
	5	2	Able Co.		300	-
Jun	30		Dr. Purch. & Cr. Acc'ts. Pay.		500	-

Purchases		No. 51	Accounts Payable		No. 21
Jun 30	500-			Jun 30	500-

Problem Using Two Journals

The following are selected transactions completed during the first week of June by The Ames Co., a retail enterprise. We are using two journals, a Purchases Journal and a General Journal. The transactions involving merchandise purchased on account are entered on one line in the Purchases Journal; all other transactions, including the one where merchandise is purchased for cash, are entered in the General Journal in the usual manner.

Jun. 1 Paul Ames invested $2,000 in new business (General Journal)

Jun. 2 Paid rent for month, $800 (General Journal)

Jun. 3 Purchased merchandise for cash, $90 (General Journal)

Jun. 4 Received Invoice No. 10 from Kilgo Co. for merchandise purchased on account, $100 (Purchases Journal)

Jun. 5 Received Invoice No. 11 from Carson Co. for merchandise purchased on account, $200 (Purchases Journal)

Jun. 7 Purchased office equipment on account, $150 (General Journal)

PURCHASES JOURNAL

Date		Inv.	From Whom Purchased		Amount	
Jun	4	10	Kilgo Co.		100	-
	5	11	Carson Co.		200	-
			Dr. Purch & Cr. Acc'ts. Pay.		300	-

GENERAL JOURNAL

Date		Description	P.F.	Debit		Credit	
Jun	1	Cash	*11*	2000 -			
		Paul Ames, Capital	*31*			2000 -	
		Initial investment					
	2	Rent Expense	*61*	800 -			
		Cash	*11*			800 -	
		Rent for month					
	3	Purchases	*51*	90 -			
		Cash	*11*			90 -	
		Bought merchandise					
	7	Office Equipment	*12*	150 -			
		Accounts Payable	*21*			150 -	
		Bought on account		3040 -		3040 -	

POSTING

Now we post from the two journals to the ledger accounts. First, we post *each amount* from the General Journal to the ledger accounts. (See pages 36 and 37). Next, we post just the total from the Purchases Journal by debiting Purchases and crediting Accounts Payable.

Cash				No. 11
Jun 1	2000-	Jun 2		800-
	_1110-_	3		90-
				_890-_

Paul Ames, Capital			No. 31
		Jun 1	2000-

Office Equipment		No. 12
Jun 7	150-	

Purchases			No. 51
Jun 3		90-	
30		300-	
	_390-_	_390-_	

Accounts Payable			No. 21
	Jun 7		150-
	30		300-
		_450-_	_450-_

Rent Expense		No. 61
Jun 2	800-	

The Ames Co.
Trial Balance
June 30

Accounts	Debit	Credit
Cash	1110 -	
Office Equipment	150 -	
Accounts Payable		450 -
Paul Ames, Capital		2000 -
Purchases	390 -	
Rent Expense	800 -	
	2450 -	2450 -

THE TRIAL BALANCE

After posting from the two journals, we foot the ledger accounts and take a Trial Balance. Note how each account is footed and the balance is entered on the larger side (see page 44). After footing each account and finding the balance, we list the balances on the Trial Balance (see above). This is to make sure the ledger is in balance.

You are to journalize the following transactions for The Carter Co. You will be using two journals—a Purchases Journal and a General Journal. Enter purchases of merchandise on account in the Purchases Journal; enter all other transactions in the General Journal.

HOMEWORK ASSIGNMENT NO. 8

Jul. 1 Jim Carter invested $1,000 in a new business
Jul. 2 Paid rent for month, $700
Jul. 3 Purchased merchandise for cash, $80
Jul. 5 Purchased merchandise on account from Kane Co., $200. Inv. No. 2
Jul. 7 Purchased merchandise on account from Goss Co., $300. Inv. No. 3
Jul. 9 Bought office Equipment on account, $250

Date	Inv.	From Whom Purchased		Amount

Date	Description	P.F.	Debit	Credit

POSTING

Post each amount from the General Journal to the ledger accounts below. Then, post just the total from the Purchases Journal. Remember, the total of the Purchases Journal is posted to two accounts in the ledger.

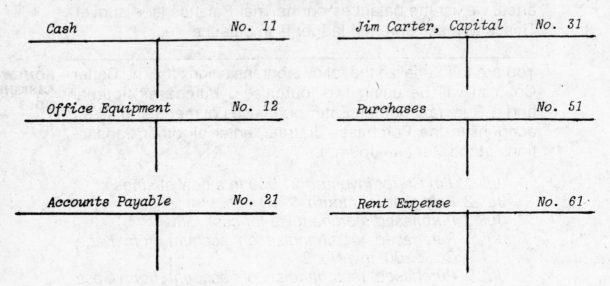

| Cash | No. 11 | Jim Carter, Capital | No. 31 |

| Office Equipment | No. 12 | Purchases | No. 51 |

| Accounts Payable | No. 21 | Rent Expense | No. 61 |

THE TRIAL BALANCE

After you have completed the posting from the two journals, foot each account in the ledger. If there is more than one amount in the account, enter the balance on the larger side. The totals, or footings, should be written in slightly smaller figures than the regular debit and credit entries. Enter the name of each account and the balances in the Trial Balance below. When you add the Trial Balance, of course, you should get the same total on each side.

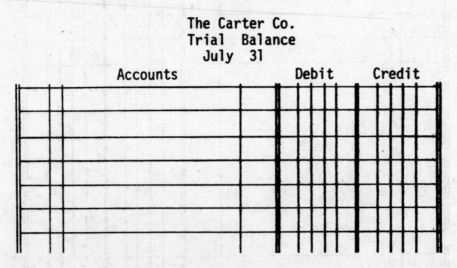

The Carter Co.
Trial Balance
July 31

| Accounts | Debit | Credit |

SELLING MERCHANDISE

The Sales Account

Selling merchandise affects a new account called Sales. When we sell merchandise for cash, the two accounts affected are Cash and Sales. Even though this is a new transaction, you should know how to record it by applying Simplified Rule 2. When we sell merchandise for cash we are receiving money; therefore, we debit Cash and credit the other account, which is Sales. This would be entered in the General Journal as follows:

June 1 Sold merchandise for cash, $100

Jun	1	Cash		1 0 0 –	
		Sales			1 0 0 –
		Sold merch. for cash			

Sales is *an income or revenue account that is always credited for the selling price.*

Sales Tax

In the foregoing illustration we omitted the *sales tax*. Most states and many cities, however, impose a retail sales tax upon the sale of tangible personal property, and this tax must be recorded as part of the sale. From now on, when we record a cash sale, we find that *three accounts are affected* instead of two. These three accounts are:

Cash
Sales
Sales Tax Payable

Let us consider this transaction.

Jun. 3 Sold merchandise for cash, amount of sale $100; sales tax $4

This transaction affects three accounts: Cash, Sales, and Sales Tax Payable. We will make *one debit and two credits*; the one debit must *equal* the two credits. We use Simplified Rule 2: Debit Cash for the money received, and credit the other two accounts. Let us analyze the transaction. How much money did we receive? We received $100 from the sale of merchandise, and we also received $4 from the customer for the sales tax. Since we received $104, we would debit Cash for $104. We would credit Sales for the selling price of $100 and, obviously, we would have to credit Sales Tax Payable for the tax of $4. This would be entered in the General Journal as follows:

Jun	3	Cash	*11*		1	0	4	–					•
		Sales	*41*							1	0	0	–
		Sales Tax Payable	*22*									4	–
		Cash sale											

Jun. 3. Sold merchandise for cash, amount of sale $100; sales tax $4

After posting the above entry from the General Journal to the General Ledger, the ledger accounts would look like this:

Cash		*No. 11*
Jun 3	104–	

Sales		*No. 41*
	Jun 3	100–

Sales Tax Payable		*No. 22*
	Jun 3	4.00

We could further analyze the transaction in the following manner:

Cash is an Asset account that is debited for the total money received, $104. (Simplified Rule 2)

Sales is an income or revenue account that is credited for the selling price, $100.

Sales Tax Payable is a Liability account that is credited for the tax collected. The tax should be credited to a liability account because we *owe the money* to the state treasurer.

Sales of Merchandise on Account

As noted previously, merchandise may be sold both for cash and on account (on credit). We learned that when we sell merchandise for cash the three accounts affected are:

Cash
Sales
Sales Tax Payable

When we sell merchandise on account, the three accounts affected are:

Accounts Receivable
Sales
Sales Tax Payable

In a charge sale, we still credit Sales for the selling price and credit Sales Tax Payable for the tax. However, since there is no cash involved at the time merchandise is sold on account, the third account affected is not Cash, but a new account called *Accounts Receivable.*

Transaction—June 9. Sold merchandise on account to Heidi Barnes. Amount of sale $100, sales tax $4

This transaction would be entered in the General Journal as follows:

Jun	9	Accounts Receivable	1 0 4 –			
		Sales			1 0 0 –	
		Sales Tax Payable				4 00
		Sold to Heidi Barnes				

Accounts Receivable is an Asset account in which we record amounts owed to us by charge customers. As shown in the foregoing General Journal entry, Accounts Receivable should be debited for the amount owed to us by the customer. Heidi Barnes owes us $100 for the merchandise sold to her, and she also owes us $4 for the sales tax. We, therefore, debit Accounts Receivable for $104, the total amount owed to us by the customer. As previously stated, we credit Sales for the selling price and credit Sales Tax Payable for the tax. Our general rule is:

When We Sell Merchandise on Account

Debit Accounts Receivable for the full amount owed to us by the customer (amount of sale plus the tax)

Credit Sales for the selling price

And credit Sales Tax Payable for the tax

THE SALES JOURNAL

We have learned how to record both cash sales and charge sales in the General Journal. However, it has been found advantageous to use a special Sales Journal in which are recorded all sales of merchandise on account. Merchandise sold for cash would still be entered in the General Journal. Following is an illustration of a typical Sales Journal.

Date	Sale No.	To Whom Sold	P F	Accounts Rec. Dr.	Sales Cr.	Sales Tax Payable Cr.

In many businesses, each charge sale is written up on a charge sales ticket or sales slip by the salesperson. The charge sales ticket is the *source document* from which the transaction is entered in the Sales Journal. You will note the following column headings in the Sales Journal:

Date   Accounts Rec. Dr.
Sale No.   Sales Cr.
To Whom Sold   Sales Tax Payable Cr.

Transaction—*June 7. Sold merchandise on account to Jane Jones, sale $100, tax $4. Sale No. 1*

This transaction would be entered in the General Journal as follows:

Date	Account	Debit	Credit
Jun 7	Accounts Receivable	104 –	
	Sales		100 –
	Sales Tax Payable		4 00
	Sold to Jane Jones		

Following our previously explained rule, we debit Accounts Receivable for $104, credit Sales for $100, and credit Sales Tax Payable for $4. Note we do exactly the same on one line in the Sales Journal.

Date	Sale No.	To Whom Sold	P F	Accounts Rec. Dr.	Sales Cr	Sales Tax Payable Cr.
Jun 7	1	Jane Jones		104 –	100 –	4 00

Just as we did in the General Journal, in the Sales Journal we debited Accounts Receivable by entering $104 in the column headed Accounts Rec. Dr.; we credited Sales by entering $100 in the column headed Sales Cr.; and we credited Sales Tax Payable by entering $4 in the column headed Sales Tax Payable Cr. We also entered the date, the sale number, and the customer's name.

Footing and Posting the Sales Journal

At the end of the month, the three columns of the Sales Journal should be footed and proved. To prove the footings, the total of the debit column should equal the sum of the two credit column totals ($208 equals $200 plus $8). After proving the totals, they should be posted to the proper accounts in the General Ledger. Note we do not post each sale individually, only the three totals. Each column total is posted as indicated by the heading of that column.

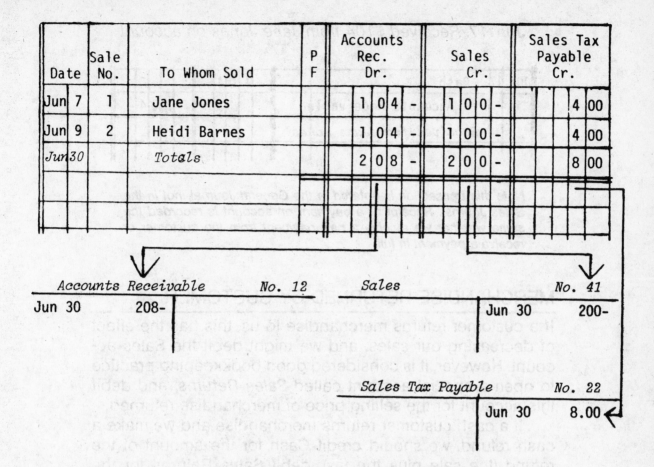

Date	Sale No.	To Whom Sold	P F	Accounts Rec. Dr.				Sales Cr.				Sales Tax Payable Cr.		
Jun 7	1	Jane Jones			1	0	4	–	1	0	0	–	4	00
Jun 9	2	Heidi Barnes			1	0	4	–	1	0	0	–	4	00
Jun 30		*Totals*			2	0	8	–	2	0	0	–	8	00

Accounts Receivable	*No. 12*		*Sales*	*No. 41*
Jun 30	208–		Jun 30	200–

Sales Tax Payable	*No. 22*
	Jun 30	8.00

Posting totals at the end of the month is called *summary posting,* and we always use the end-of-the-month date.

RECEIVING PAYMENTS FROM CUSTOMERS

Payments are received periodically from charge customers as their accounts become due. Receiving money from a charge customer affects two accounts: Cash and Accounts Receivable. We use Simplified Rule 2: When we receive money, always debit Cash and credit the other account; therefore, we debit Cash and credit Accounts Receivable. This transaction would appear in the General Journal as follows:

Jun. 17. Received $104 from Jane Jones on account

Jun 17	Cash		1 0 4 –		
	Accounts Receivable			1 0 4 –	
	Received from Jane Jones				

Note this transaction is entered in the General Journal, not in the Sales Journal. Receipt of a payment on account is recorded the same whether we receive a part payment from the customer or receive a payment in full.

MERCHANDISE RETURNED BY CUSTOMER

If a customer returns merchandise to us, this has the effect of decreasing our sales, and we might debit the Sales account. However, it is considered good bookkeeping practice to open a special account called *Sales Returns,* and debit this account for the selling price of merchandise returned.

If a cash customer returns merchandise and we make a cash refund, we should credit Cash for the amount of the refund (the sale plus the tax), debit Sales Returns for the selling price, and debit Sales Tax Payable for the tax.

If a charge customer returns merchandise, we should again debit Sales Returns for the selling price, debit Sales Tax Payable for the tax, and credit Accounts Receivable for the total. These two transactions would be entered in the General Journal as follows:

> *Jun. 5. Customer returned merchandise and we made a cash refund. Selling price was $100 and tax was $4*
> *Jun. 11. Heidi Barnes returned merchandise for credit. Sale $100, tax $4*

Jun	5	Sales Returns				1	0	0	-						
		Sales Tax Payable						4	00						
		Cash								1	0	4	-		
		Made cash refund													
Jun	11	Sales Returns				1	0	0	-						
		Sales Tax Payable						4	00						
		Accounts Receivable								1	0	4	-		
		Heidi Barnes ret. merch.													

It should be noted that Accounts Receivable is an Asset account that is debited for any increase, such as a charge sale (amount of sale plus the tax). The account should be credited for any decrease, such as receiving a payment from a customer, or a customer returning merchandise for credit.

Problem Using Two Journals

The following are selected transactions completed during June by The Acme Co., a retail enterprise. We are using two journals, a General Journal and a Sales Journal. The transactions involving merchandise sold on account are entered in the Sales Journal; all other transactions, including cash sales, are entered in the General Journal in the usual manner.

> Jun. 1. James Acme invested $3000 in a new business (General Journal)
>
> Jun. 2. Paid June rent, $800 (General Journal)
>
> Jun. 3. Sold merchandise for cash, $100, sales tax $4 (General Journal)
>
> Jun. 4. Sold merchandise on account to J.R. Adams, $200, sales tax $8, sale No. 101 (Sales Journal)
>
> Jun. 5. Sold merchandise on account to James Cox, $300, sales tax $12, sale No. 102 (Sales Journal)
>
> Jun. 30. Received check for $208 from J.R. Adams on account (General Journal)

Date	Sale No.	To Whom Sold	P F	Accounts Rec. Dr.			Sales Cr.			Sales Tax Payable Cr.		
Jun 4	101	J. R. Adams		2	0	8 -	2	0	0 -		8	00
5	102	James Cox		3	1	2 -	3	0	0 -		1 2	00
Jun 30		Totals		5	2	0 -	5	0	0 -		2 0	00

Date	Description	P.F.	Debit				Credit			
Jun 1	Cash		3	0	0	0 -				
	James Acme, Capital						3	0	0	0 -
	Invested in new business									
Jun 2	Rent Expense			8	0	0 -				
	Cash							8	0	0 -
	June rent									
Jun 3	Cash			1	0	4 -				
	Sales							1	0	0 -
	Sales Tax Payable								4	00
	Cash sales									
Jun 30	Cash			2	0	8 -				
	Accounts Receivable							2	0	8 -
	From J.R. Adams on acc't.									

Posting

We post every amount from the General Journal to the ledger accounts in the usual manner. Then we post the three totals from the Sales Journal. The totals are posted as indicated by the column headings—the $520 is posted to the debit of Accounts Receivable; the $500 is posted to the credit of Sales; the $20 is posted to the credit of Sales Tax Payable.

Cash				No. 11
Jun 1	3000-	Jun 2	800-	
3	104-			
30	208-			

James Acme, Capital			No. 31
		Jun 1	3000-

Accounts Receivable				No. 12
Jun 30	520-	Jun 30	208-	

Sales			No. 41
		Jun 3	100-
		30	500-

Sales Tax Payable			No. 22
		Jun 3	4.00
		30	20.00

Rent Expense		No. 61
Jun 2	800-	

Record the following June transactions for the Dodge Co. in the two journals following. Enter all charge sales in the Sales Journal; enter all other transactions, including cash sales, in the General Journal.

HOMEWORK ASSIGNMENT NO. 9

Jun. 1. Joe Dodge invested $4000 in a new business
Jun. 2. Paid June rent, $900
Jun. 3. Sold merchandise for cash, $200, sales tax $8
Jun. 4. Sold merchandise on account to J. S. Brown, $300, sales tax $12
Jun. 5. Sold merchandise on account to A. B. Fuller, $400, sales tax $16

Date	Description	P.F.	Debit	Credit

Date	Sale No.	To Whom Sold	P F	Accounts Rec. Dr.	Sales Cr.	Sales Tax Payable Cr.

Post *every figure* from the General Journal to the ledger accounts following. Then post the three totals from the Sales Journal as indicated by the column headings. Use the June 30 date when posting the totals.

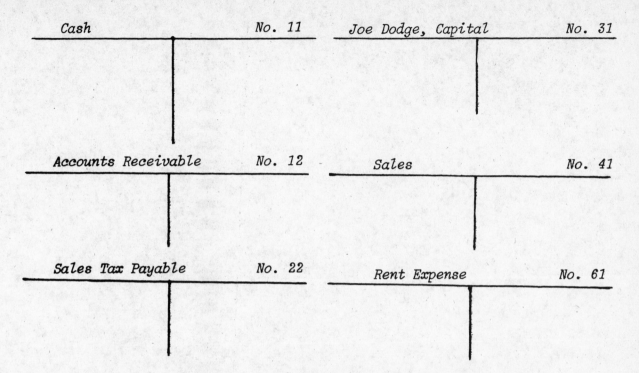

Cash   No. 11   Joe Dodge, Capital   No. 31

Accounts Receivable   No. 12   Sales   No. 41

Sales Tax Payable   No. 22   Rent Expense   No. 61

Trial Balance

Foot each ledger account and find the balance for each account, then list each account and its balance on the Trial Balance form below (see pages 44–45).

The Dodge Co.
Trial Balance

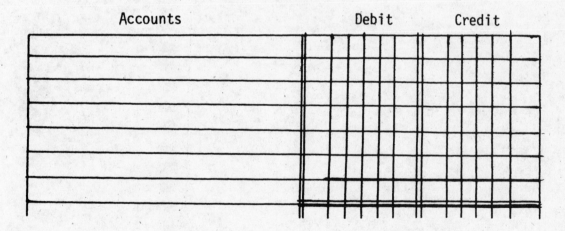

Accounts	Debit	Credit

The Eight-Column Combined Cash Journal

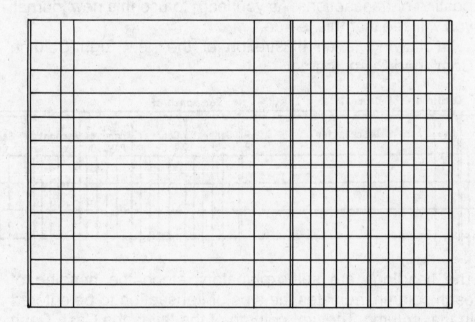

So far we have learned how to record transactions in four
different journals—the General Journal, the Four-Column
Cash Journal, the Purchases Journal, and the Sales Journal.
As we have often stated, any transaction can be recorded in
a General Journal. However, we have also seen that the use
of special journals, such as a Purchases Journal and a
Sales Journal, facilitates the journalizing and posting of
certain transactions.

Another special journal is the *Eight-Column Combined
Cash Journal,* which we will learn to use next. We will still
use a Purchases Journal to record all purchases of merchandise on account, and we will still use a Sales Journal to
record all sales of merchandise on account. *All other transactions* will be entered in the new Eight-Column Combined
Cash Journal.

It should be noted once again that the *only* reason for
using this new special journal in place of the General
Journal is because it greatly facilitates the journalizing and
posting of transactions. As you learn to use this new journal,
you will see that this is true.

Following is an illustration of the new Eight-Column
Combined Cash Journal.

Combined Cash Journal   For Month Of

Cash Dr.	Cash Cr.	Day	Description	P R	General Dr.	General Cr.	Accounts Pay. Dr.	Accounts Rec. Cr.	Sales Cr.	Sales .Tx Pay. Cr

The headings are self-explanatory, since the heading of
each column indicates the type of transaction to be entered
in that column. The first column at the left is the Cash Debit
column, and the second column is the Cash Credit column.
Next come the Day, Description, and P.R. (Posting Reference) columns. Next, in order, are the General Debit column,

General Credit, Accounts Payable Debit, Accounts Receivable Credit, Sales Credit, and Sales Tax Payable Credit.

We will now consider several selected transactions and show exactly how to enter each one in the Combined Cash Journal. In recording transactions in the Combined Cash Journal, we use our Three Simplified Rules: 1. When we pay out money, always credit Cash and debit the other account. 2. When we receive money, always debit Cash and credit the other account. 3. When we buy equipment on account, always debit Equipment and credit Accounts Payable.

Jun. 1. Paid $50 on account to Rogers Co.
This transaction affects Cash and Accounts Payable. Use Rule 1: Credit Cash and debit Accounts Payable. The transaction would be entered this way in the General Journal:

Jun	1	Accounts Payable			5 0	-				
		Cash					5 0	-		
		Paid Rogers Co. on acc't.								

The same transaction appears like this when entered in the Combined Cash Journal:

Combined Cash Journal   For Month Of *JUNE*

Cash Dr.	Cash Cr.	Day	Description	P R	General Dr.	General Cr.	Accounts Pay. Dr.	Accounts Rec. Cr.	Sales Cr.	Sales .Tx Pay. Cr
	5 0 -	1	Rogers Co.				5 0 -			

Notice the way we credit Cash is to enter $50 in the second column at the left, which is the Cash Cr. column. The way we debit Accounts Payable is to enter $50 in the third column on the right, which is headed Accounts Pay. Dr. Just entering the $50 in these two particular columns indicates we are crediting Cash and debiting Accounts Payable. Then we enter the date in the Day column and write "Rogers Co." in the Description column. So we see, any time we need to credit Cash, we enter the amount in the Cash Cr. column, which is the second column at the left. Any time we need to debit Accounts Payable, we enter the amount in the third column on the right.

Jun. 2. Received $75 on account from J. R. Jones
This transaction affects Cash and Accounts Receivable. Use Rule 2: Debit Cash and credit Accounts Receivable. The transaction is entered this way in the General Journal:

Jun	2	Cash			75	-		
		Accounts Receivable					75	-
		J. R. Jones on acc't.						

The same transaction is entered this way in the Combined Cash Journal:

			Combined Cash Journal				For Month Of *JUNE*				
Cash Dr.	Cash Cr.	Day	Description	P R	General Dr.	General Cr.	Accounts Pay. Dr.	Accounts Rec. Cr.	Sales Cr.	Sales .Tx Pay. Cr
75-		2	J. R. Jones					75-		

Notice the way we debit Cash is to enter $75 in the first column at the left, which is the Cash Dr. column. The way we credit Accounts Receivable is to enter the $75 in the fourth column on the right, which is headed Accounts Rec. Cr. Entering the $75 in these two particular columns indicates we are debiting Cash and crediting Accounts Receivable. We enter the date in the Day column and write J. R. Jones in the Description column. So we see, any time we need to debit Cash, we enter the amount in the Cash Dr. column, which is the first column at the left. Any time we need to credit Accounts Receivable, we enter the amount in the fourth column on the right.

Jun. 3. Sold merchandise for cash. Sale $100, sales tax $4 This transaction affects three accounts: Cash, Sales, and Sales Tax Payable. Use Rule 2: Debit Cash, credit Sales, and credit Sales Tax Payable. The transaction is entered this way in the General Journal:

Jun	3	Cash	104 –		
		Sales		100 –	
		Sales Tax Payable			400
		Cash sales			

The same transaction is entered this way in the Combined Cash Journal:

Cash Dr.	Cash Cr.	Day	Description	P R	General Dr.	General Cr.	Accounts Pay. Dr.	Accounts Rec. Cr.	Sales Cr.	Sales .Tx Pay. Cr
104		3	Cash sales						100–	4–

Combined Cash Journal   For Month Of JUNE

The way we debit Cash is to enter the $104 in the first column at the left. The way we credit Sales is to enter the amount of the sale, $100, in the fifth column on the right. The way we credit Sales Tax Payable is to enter the $4 in the last column on the right. Making entries in these three particular columns indicates we are debiting Cash, crediting Sales, and crediting Sales Tax Payable. We enter the date and write "Cash sales" in the Description column. Notice this transaction required *four* lines in the General Journal, but can be entered on just *one line* in the Combined Cash Journal. This graphically illustrates one of the advantages of using a Combined Cash Journal instead of the General Journal.

Jun. 5. Paid June rent, $500

This transaction affects Cash and Rent Expense. Use Rule 1: Credit Cash and debit Rent Expense. The transaction is entered this way in the General Journal:

Jun	5	Rent Expense		5 0 0 –		
		Cash			5 0 0 –	
		Paid June rent				

The same transaction is entered this way in the Combined Cash Journal:

Cash Dr.	Cash Cr.	Day	Description	P R	General Dr.	General Cr.	Accounts Pay. Dr.	Accounts Rec. Cr.	Sales Cr.	Sales .Tx Pay. Cr
	5 0 0 –	5	Rent Expense		5 0 0 –					

Combined Cash Journal   For Month Of *JUNE*

The way we credit Cash is to enter $500 in the second column at the left. We do not have a special column headed Rent Expense Dr.; therefore, we write Rent Expense in the Description column and debit it in the General Dr. column.

Following are the foregoing transactions all entered in one Combined Cash Journal.

Cash Dr.	Cash Cr.	Day	Description	P R	General Dr.	General Cr.	Accounts Pay. Dr.	Accounts Rec. Cr.	Sales Cr.	Sales Tx Pay. Cr.
	50-	1	Rogers Co.				50-			
75-		2	J. R. Jones					75-		
104-		3	Cash sales						100-	4-
	500-	5	Rent Expense		500-					
179-	550-	30	*Totals*		500-		50-	75-	100-	4-

POSTING FROM THE COMBINED CASH JOURNAL

Cash	No. 11		*Accounts Payable*	No. 21		*Sales*	No. 41
Jun 30 179-	Jun 30 550-		Jun 30 50-				Jun 30 100-

Accounts Receivable	No. 12		*Sales Tax Payable*	No. 22		*Rent Expense*	No. 61
	Jun 30 75-			Jun 30 4.00		Jun 5 500-	

Proving the Footings

At the end of the month, all columns should be footed and the footings should be proved. To prove the footings, list the totals from all the debit columns (Cash Dr., General Dr., Accounts Payable Dr.) and add them; then list the totals from all the credit columns (Cash Cr., Accounts Rec. Cr., Sales Cr., Sales Tax Pay. Cr.) and add them. The totals of the two lists should be equal.

Proof of Footings

Debit Columns		*Credit Columns*	
Cash Dr.	$179.00	Cash Cr.	$550.00
General Dr.	500.00	Accounts Rec. Cr.	75.00
Accounts Pay. Dr.	50.00	Sales Cr.	100.00
	729.00	Sales Tax Pay. Cr.	4.00
			729.00

In posting from the Combined Cash Journal, a considerable saving in time and effort is effected because we post only the totals of all columns (except the General Dr. and General Cr. columns). The proper procedure is to post, first of all, each amount from the two General columns. The amounts are posted to the accounts indicated in the Description column; therefore, we post the $500 from the General Dr. column as a debit to Rent Expense on June 5 (see above). There is no amount in the General Cr. column to be posted. Next, we post the totals of all other columns as indicated by the column headings. In posting the totals, which is called summary posting, we use the date of June 30.

The $179 is posted as a debit to Cash; the $550 is posted as a credit to Cash; the $50 is posted as a debit to Accounts Payable; the $75 is posted as a credit to Accounts Receivable; the $100 is posted as a credit to Sales; and the $4 is posted as a credit to Sales Tax Payable.

Once again, the procedure for posting from the Combined Cash Journal is to post each amount from the two General columns first; then post the totals from all other columns, as indicated by the column headings.

COMPLETE PROBLEM

In this exercise we will record the transactions for an entire month for a typical retail enterprise, The Smith Store.

As the books of original entry, The Smith Store uses a Purchases Journal for recording all merchandise purchased on account; a Sales Journal for recording all merchandise sold on account; and an Eight-Column Combined Cash Journal for recording *all other* transactions.

The General Ledger for The Smith Store consists of the following accounts:

Cash	Sales Tax Payable	Purchases
Accounts Receivable	Sam Smith, Capital	Rent Expense
Office Equipment	Sam Smith, Drawing	Advertising
Accounts Payable	Sales	Expense

Read each transaction carefully. Note in which journal each transaction is entered and how it is entered in that journal. Remember we use the Three Simplified Rules:

1. When we pay out money, always credit Cash and debit the other account.
2. When we receive money, always debit Cash and credit the other account.
3. When we buy equipment on account, debit Equipment and credit Accounts Payable.

> *Jun. 1. Owner invested $5,000 cash in new business*
> (Cash Journal. Dr. Cash and Cr. Sam Smith, Capital)
> *Jun. 1. Paid June rent, $800*
> (Cash Journal. Cr. Cash and Dr. Rent Expense)
> *Jun. 2. Purchase merchandise on account from Barton Co., $900*
> (Enter in Purchases Journal)
> *Jun. 3. Sold merchandise on account to S.E. Dayton, sale $100, tax $4*
> (Enter in Sales Journal)
> *Jun. 5. Purchased merchandise for cash, $700*
> (Cash Journal. Cr. Cash and Dr. Purchases)

Jun. 7. Sold merchandise for cash, sale $200, tax $8
(Cash Journal. Dr. Cash, Cr. Sales, and Cr. Sales Tax Payable)

Jun. 15. Purchased merchandise on account from Cole Co., $500
(Enter in Purchases Journal)

Jun. 17. Purchased new office desk from Shaw Co. on account, $325
(Cash Journal. Dr. Office Equipment and Cr. Accounts Payable. Note this transaction requires two lines in Cash Journal)

Jun. 21. Sam Smith, the owner, withdrew $125 for personal use
(Cash Journal. Cr. Cash and Dr. Sam Smith, Drawing)

Jun. 22. Sold merchandise on account to Paul Barnes, sale $300, tax $12
(Enter in Sales Journal)

Jun. 23. Paid Shaw Co. $225 on account
(Cash Journal. Cr. Cash and Dr. Accounts Payable)

Jun. 28. Paid advertising bill, $150
(Cash Journal. Cr. Cash and Dr. Advertising Expense)

Jun. 30. Received $104 cash on account from S.E. Dayton
(Cash Journal. Dr. Cash and Cr. Accounts Receivable)

PURCHASES JOURNAL

Date		Inv.	From Whom Purchased		Amount	
Jun	2	1	Barton Co.		900	-
	15	2	Cole Co.		500	-
Jun	30		Dr. Purch. & Cr. Acc'ts. Pay.		1400	-

Combined Cash Journal

For Month Of JUNE

Cash Dr.	Cash Cr.	Day	Description	PR	General Dr.	General Cr.	Accounts Pay. Dr.	Accounts Rec. Cr.	Sales Cr.	Sales Tx Pay. Cr.
5000 -		1	Sam Smith, Capital	31		5000 -				
	800 -	1	Rent Expense	61	800 -					
	700 -	5	Purchases	51	700 -					
208 -		7	Cash sales	✓					200 -	8 -
		17	Office Equipment	14	325 -					
			Accounts Payable	21		325 -	225 -			
	125 -	21	Sam Smith, Drawing	031	125 -					
	225 -	23	Shaw Co. on account	✓			225 -			
	150 -	28	Advertising Expense	63	150 -					
104 -		30	From S.E. Dayton on account	✓				104 -		
5312 -	2000 -	30	Totals		2100 -	5325 -	225 -	104 -	200 -	8 -

Sales Journal

Date	Sale No.	To Whom Sold	PF	Accounts Rec. Dr.	Sales Cr.	Sales Tax Payable Cr.
Jun 3	1	S. E. Dayton		104 -	100 -	4 00
22	2	Paul Barnes		312 -	300 -	12 00
Jun 30		Totals		416 -	400 -	16 00

POSTING PROCEDURE

Keep referring to pages 99 and 101 as we explain the proper procedure for posting to the ledger accounts on page 103. When posting from the Combined Cash Journal (page 101), we first posted each figure from the *two general columns.* The first amount in the two general columns is $5,000. This was posted as a credit to Sam Smith, Capital. The $800 was posted as a debit to Rent Expense. The $700 was posted as a debit to Purchases. The first $325 was posted as a debit to Office Equipment. The other $325 was posted as a credit to Accounts Payable. The $125 was posted as a debit to Sam Smith, Drawing. The $150 was posted as a debit to Advertising Expense. That completed the posting from the two General columns.

Next, we posted the totals of all other columns in the Combined Cash Journal. The $5,312 was posted as a debit to Cash. The $2,000 was posted as a credit to Cash. (We do not post the two general column totals, since we have already posted each amount from those two columns.) The $225 was posted as a debit to Accounts Payable. The $104 was posted as a credit to Accounts Receivable. The $200 was posted as a credit to Sales. The $8 was posted as a credit to Sales Tax Payable. That completed the posting from the Combined Cash Journal.

Next, we posted the three totals from the Sales Journal. These were posted as indicated by the column headings. The $416 was posted as a debit to Accounts Receivable. The $400 was posted as a credit to Sales. The $16 was posted as a credit to Sales Tax Payable.

Last, we posted the total from the Purchases Journal. This total, $1,400, was posted as a debit to Purchases and a credit to Accounts Payable.

THE SMITH STORE - GENERAL LEDGER

Cash		No. 11
Jun 30	5312-	Jun 30	2000-
3312-			

Sam Smith, Drawing		No. 031
Jun 21	125-	
125-		

Accounts Receivable		No. 12
Jun 30	416-	Jun 30	104-
312-			

Sales		No. 41
	Jun 30	200-
	30 *600-*	400- *600-*

Office Equipment		No. 14
Jun 17	325-	
325		

Purchases		No. 51
Jun 5	700-	
30	1400-	
2100- 2100-		

Accounts Payable		No. 21
Jun 30	225-	Jun 17	325-
		30	1400-
		1500- 1725-	

Rent Expense		No. 61
Jun 1	800-	
800-		

Sales Tax Payable		No. 22
	Jun 30	8.00
	30	16.00
	24-	*24.00*

Advertising Expense		No. 62
Jun 28 *150-*	150-	

Sam Smith, Capital		No. 31
	Jun 1	5000-
	5000-	

THE TRIAL BALANCE

After posting from the Combined Cash Journal, the Sales Journal, and the Purchases Journal, we footed the ledger accounts and determined the balance of each account. We then took a Trial Balance on the form below to make sure the ledger was in balance.

Refer to pages 44, 45 and 46 for the proper procedure for finding the balances and taking a Trial Balance.

The Smith Store
Trial Balance
June 30

Account	Debit	Credit
Cash	3 3 1 2 -	
Accounts Receivable	3 1 2 -	
Office Equipment	3 2 5 -	
Accounts Payable		1 5 0 0 -
Sales Tax Payable		2 4 -
Sam Smith, Capital		5 0 0 0 -
Sam Smith, Drawing	1 2 5 -	
Sales		6 0 0 -
Purchases	2 1 0 0 -	
Rent Expense	8 0 0 -	
Advertising Expense	1 5 0 -	
	7 1 2 4 -	7 1 2 4 -

Notice in this problem we worked through the complete Bookkeeping Cycle for one month, which consisted of the following steps: 1. Journalize the transactions, using a Purchases Journal, a Sales Journal, and a Combined Cash Journal. 2. Total the journals and prove the footings. 3. Post from all three journals to the ledger accounts. 4. Foot the ledger accounts, ascertain the balance of each account, and take a Trial Balance.

For this homework assignment you will record the transactions for an entire month for The Walker Store. You will use three journals. All transactions involving merchandise purchased on account will be entered in the Purchases Journal; all charge sales will be entered in the Sales Journal; all other transactions will be entered in the Combined Cash Journal. The General Ledger for The Walker Store consists of the following accounts:

Cash	Sales Tax Payable	Rent Expense
Accounts Receivable	Wayne Walker, Capital	Electric
Office Equipment	Sales	Expense
Accounts Payable	Purchases	

Remember the Three Simplified Rules: 1. When we pay out money, always credit Cash and debit the other account. 2. When we receive money, always debit Cash and credit the other account. 3. When we buy equipment on account, debit Equipment and credit Accounts Payable.

> *Note: When you can do this assignment correctly, and understand it,* you have mastered the recording phase of basic bookkeeping and accounting!

Jul. 1. Owner invested $6,000 cash in new business
Jul. 1. Paid July rent, $900
Jul. 2. Purchased merchandise on account from Grimes Co., $700
Jul. 3. Sold merchandise on account to B. A. Hall, sale $100, tax $4
Jul. 5. Purchased merchandise for cash, $800
Jul. 7. Sold merchandise for cash, sale $200, tax $8
Jul. 15. Purchased merchandise on account from Hames Co., $400
Jul. 17. Purchased new office desk from Lane Co. on account, $300
Jul. 22. Sold merchandise on account to Jay Reed, sale $400, tax $16
Jul. 23. Paid Grimes Co. $200 on account
Jul. 28. Paid electric bill, $78
Jul. 30. Received $104 cash on account from B. A. Hall

PURCHASES JOURNAL

Date	Inv.	From Whom Purchased		Amount

Combined Cash Journal

For Month of JULY

Cash Dr.	Cash Cr.	Day	Description	P R	General Dr.	General Cr.	Accounts Payb. Dr.	Accounts Rec. Cr.	Sales Cr.	Sales Tx Pay. Cr.

Date	Sale No.	To Whom Sold	P F	Accounts Rec. Dr.	Sales Cr.	Sales Tax Payable Cr.

HOME-WORK NO. 10 CONTINUED -- THE WALKER STORE GENERAL LEDGER ACCOUNTS

Cash   No. 11

Accounts Payable   No. 21

Sales   No. 41

Accounts Receivable   No. 12

Sales Tax Payable   No. 22

Purchases   No. 51

Office Equipment   No. 14

Wayne Walker, Capital   No. 31

Rent Expense   No. 61

Electric Expense   No. 63

Posting

Total all three journals and prove the footings of the Combined Cash Journal and the Sales Journal. Then, post from the three journals to the ledger accounts on this page (refer to page 102).

The Trial Balance

After posting from the three journals to the ledger accounts, foot the ledger accounts and find the balance for each account. Enter the balance on the larger side of each account (refer to pages 44, 45, and 46). Take a Trial Balance on the form below.

THE WALKER STORE
TRIAL BALANCE
JULY 31

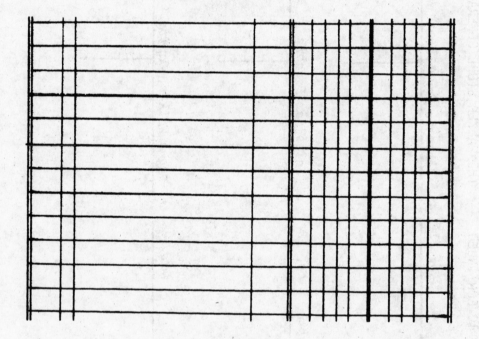

LESSON SEVEN

Subsidiary Ledgers

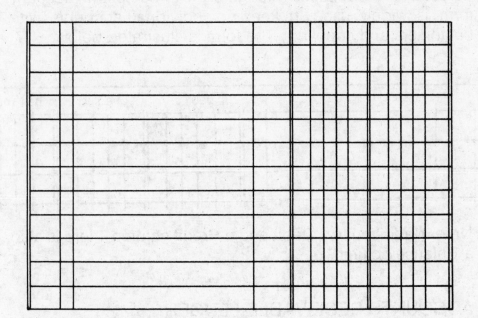

In many business enterprises, where the volume of certain transactions warrants it, an *Accounts Receivable Ledger* and an *Accounts Payable Ledger* are maintained. These are known as *subsidiary ledgers,* meaning they are subsidiary to or in addition to the General Ledger.

The Accounts Receivable Ledger consists of a separate ledger account with each customer to whom we sell merchandise on credit. The Accounts Payable Ledger consists of a separate ledger account with each individual or supplier from whom we buy on credit.

ACCOUNT FORM FOR THE SUBSIDIARY LEDGER

We are already familiar with the standard T ledger account used for General Ledger accounts. Although this form could be used for the subsidiary ledgers, the *three-column account form* is widely used in keeping individual accounts with customers and suppliers. The form is illustrated below.

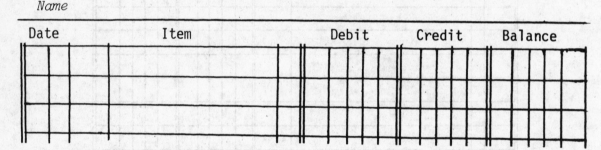

Note in addition to a Debit and a Credit column, there is also a Balance column.

ACCOUNTS RECEIVABLE LEDGER

As previously explained, the Accounts Receivable Ledger consists of a separate account with each customer to whom we sell merchandise on credit. Since charge sales are always entered in the Sales Journal, we would have an account for each name recorded in the Sales Journal. There are three kinds of transactions that affect accounts with customers in the subsidiary Accounts Receivable Ledger, namely:

1. *When we sell merchandise on account.* This transaction is entered in the Sales Journal, and we post the full amount owed to us as a debit to the customer's account in the Accounts Receivable Ledger.
2. *When we receive a payment from a customer to apply on account.* This transaction is entered in the Combined Cash Journal as a debit to Cash and a credit to Accounts Receivable. The amount is then posted as a credit to the customer's account in the Accounts Receivable Ledger.
3. *When merchandise is returned to us for credit by a charge customer.* This transaction is entered in the Combined Cash Journal as a debit to Sales Returns and a credit to Accounts Receivable (see page 84). The amount is then posted as a credit to the customer's account in the Accounts Receivable Ledger.

Following are illustrations of the foregoing transactions.

Jun. 5. Sold merchandise on account to Sally Summers, sale $300, tax $12

This would be entered in the Sales Journal as follows:

Date	Sale No.	To Whom Sold	P F	Accounts Rec. Dr.	Sales Cr.	Sales Tax Payable Cr.
Jun 5	1	Sally Summers		3 1 2 –	3 0 0 –	1 2 0 0

As soon as a charge sale is entered in the Sales Journal, it is customary to post the transaction immediately to the customer's account in the Accounts Receivable Ledger. By following this procedure, the balance in the customer's account is kept up to date. We post the amount from the first column of the Sales Journal, which is the amount owed to us by the customer. This column is headed "Accounts Rec. Dr."; therefore, we post $312 as a debit to Sally Summers's account and also enter the balance in the Balance Column, as follows:

Name   Sally Summers

Date		Item	Debit	Credit	Balance
Jun	5		3 1 2 –		3 1 2 –

Jun. 15. Received $100 from Sally Summers on account
This would be entered in the Combined Cash Journal as
follows:

Combined Cash Journal   For Month Of *JUNE*

Cash Dr.	Cash Cr.	Day	Description	P R	General Dr.	General Cr.	Accounts Pay. Dr.	Accounts Rec. Cr.
1 0 0 –		15	Sally Summers					1 0 0 –

We should immediately post the $100 as a credit to Sally
Summers's account:

Name   Sally Summers

Date		Item	Debit	Credit	Balance
Jun	5		3 1 2 –		3 1 2 –
	15			1 0 0 –	2 1 2 –

Note that when we posted the $100 credit we subtracted from
the previous balance and entered the new balance, $212, in
the Balance column.

> *Jun. 20. Sally Summers returned merchandise to us for credit $20*

This would be entered in the Combined Cash Journal on June 20:

Combined Cash Journal   For Month Of **JUNE**

Cash Dr.	Cash Cr.	Day	Description	P R	General Dr.	General Cr.	Accounts Pay. Dr.	Accounts Rec. Cr.
		20	Sales Returns (S. Summers)		20 -			20 -

We should immediately post the $20 as a credit to Sally Summers's account, as follows:

Name   Sally Summers

Date		Item	Debit	Credit	Balance
Jun	5		3 1 2 -		3 1 2 -
	15			1 0 0 -	2 1 2 -
	20			2 0 -	1 9 2 -

Note that we subtracted the $20 credit from the previous balance and entered the new balance, $192, in the Balance column. This is the amount the customer owes us as of June 20.

Remember, at the end of the month we still post the totals from the Sales Journal and from the Combined Cash Journal to the General Ledger accounts; we post to the customer's accounts in the subsidiary Accounts Receivable Ledger on a daily basis.

ACCOUNTS PAYABLE LEDGER

As previously noted, the Accounts Payable Ledger consists of a separate account for each individual or supplier from whom we buy on credit. Items purchased on credit consist mainly of merchandise, equipment, and supplies. Transactions involving the purchase of merchandise on account are entered in the Purchases Journal; therefore, we would open an account with each creditor recorded in the Purchases Journal. Transactions involving the purchase of equipment or supplies on account are entered in the Combined Cash Journal, and an account would also be opened with each of these creditors. There are four kinds of transactions that affect accounts with creditors in the subsidiary Accounts Payable Ledger, namely:

1. *When we purchase merchandise on account.* This transaction is entered in the Purchases Journal and should be posted as a credit to the Accounts Payable Ledger.
2. *When we buy equipment on account.* This transaction is entered in the Combined Cash Journal and should be posted as a credit to the Account Payable Ledger.
3. *When we make a payment on account to a creditor.* This transaction is entered in the Combined Cash Journal and should be posted as a debit to the Accounts Payable Ledger.
4. *When we return an item to the supplier for credit.* This transaction is entered in the Combined Cash Journal and should be posted as a debit to the Accounts Payable Ledger.

The following are illustrations of the foregoing transactions:

Jun. 5. Purchased merchandise on account from The Smith Co., $150

This would be entered in the Purchases Journal as follows:

PURCHASES JOURNAL

Date		Inv.	From Whom Purchased		Amount	
Jun	5		The Smith Co.		150	–

It should be posted as a credit to The Smith Co. account in the Accounts Payable Ledger as follows:

Name The Smith Co.

Date	Item	Debit	Credit	Balance
Jun 5			1 5 0 -	1 5 0 -

Jun. 6. Bought office equipment on account from The Shaw Co., $500

This would be entered in the Combined Cash Journal as follows:

Combined Cash Journal   For Month Of *JUNE*

Cash Dr.	Cash Cr.	Day	Description	P R	General Dr.	General Cr.	Accounts Pay. Dr.	Acco Rec
		6	Office Equipment		5 0 0 -			
			Accounts Payable *(Shaw Co.)*			5 0 0 -		

It should be posted as a credit to The Shaw Co. account:

Name The Shaw Co.

Date	Item	Debit	Credit	Balance
Jun 6			5 0 0 -	5 0 0 -

Jun. 9. Paid The Smith Co. $50 on account
This would be entered in the Combined Cash Journal as follows:

Combined Cash Journal   For Month Of

Cash Dr.	Cash Cr.	Day	Description	PR	General Dr.	General Cr.	Accounts Pay. Dr.	Accou Rec
		6	Office Equipment		500-			
			Accounts Payable *(Shaw Co.)*			500-		
	50-	9	*Smith Co. on account*				50-	

It should be posted to The Smith Co. account as follows:

Name   The Smith Co.

Date		Item		Debit	Credit	Balance
Jun	5				150-	150-
	9			50-		100-

Note that we subtracted the $50 debit from the previous balance and entered the new balance, $100, in the Balance column.

Jun. 12. Returned some merchandise to The Smith Co. for credit, $25

This transaction should be entered in the Combined Cash Journal as follows (see pages 69 and 70):

Combined Cash Journal   For Month Of *JUNE*

Cash Dr.	Cash Cr.	Day	Description	P R	General Dr.	General Cr.	Accounts Pay. Dr.	Accou Rec.
		6	Office Equipment		500-			
			Accounts Payable *(Shaw Co.)*			500-		
	50-	9	*Smith Co. on account*				50-	
		12	Purchases Returns *(Smith Co.)*			25-	25-	

It should be posted to The Smith Co. account as follows:

Name   The Smith Co.

Date		Item	Debit	Credit	Balance
Jun	5			150-	150-
	9		50-		100-
	12		25-		75-

Note that we subtracted the $25 debit from the previous balance and entered the new balance, $75, in the Balance column. This is the amount we owe The Smith Co. as of June 12.

Remember, at the end of the month we still post the totals from the Purchases Journal and from the Combined Cash Journal to the General Ledger accounts; we post to the accounts in the subsidiary Accounts Payable Ledger on a daily basis.

LESSON EIGHT

Financial Statements

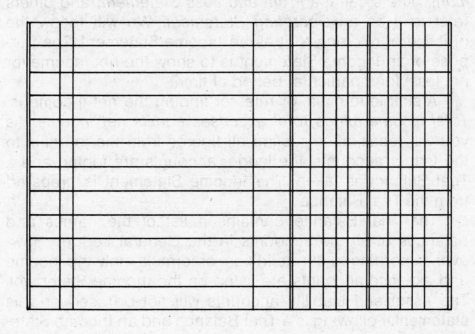

A set of bookkeeping records is maintained to fill several different needs. So far, we have learned how to record correctly, in different journals, the day-to-day transactions of a business enterprise. In addition, in order to operate a business intelligently and profitably, the owners and operators of the business require various reports and *financial statements.* These are prepared from the bookkeeping records. Depending on the nature and needs of the business, these reports may be prepared monthly, quarterly, or at the end of the year. The two most important of these financial statements are the *Income Statement* and the *Balance Sheet.*

THE INCOME STATEMENT

Some accountants refer to this report as an *Income Statement,* others call it a *Profit and Loss Statement,* and others refer to it as an *Operating Statement.* We will follow the practice of referring to it as an Income Statement. The purpose of an Income Statement is to show the net income (or net loss) for a particular period of time.

A simple formula, or rule, for finding the net income is: *Total income minus total expenses equals net income.* As you will recall, after posting all figures from the journals to the ledger accounts, the ledger accounts are footed and a Trial Balance is taken. The Income Statement is prepared from the Trial Balance.

The Trial Balance contains a list of the names and balances of all the accounts in the General Ledger. However, according to our definition, or formula, only the income and expense accounts are listed on the Income Statement. The Asset and Liability accounts will not be used on this statement. Following is a Trial Balance and an Income Statement prepared on two-column paper from the Trial Balance. The two amount columns on the Income Statement are *not* debit and credit columns; they are simply two columns in which the figures are arranged conveniently for adding and subtracting. We use a three-line heading for the statement.

Trial Balance
June 30

	Debit	Credit
Cash	4 8 9 7 -	
Office Equipment	7 3 0 -	
Accounts Payable		3 3 0 -
George Van, Capital		5 0 0 0 -
Income From Fees		1 0 0 0 -
Rent Expense	6 0 0 -	
Telephone Expense	3 8 -	
Truck Expense	6 5 -	
	6 3 3 0 -	6 3 3 0 -

George Van Moving Co.
Income Statement
June 30

Income		
Income From Fees	1 0 0 0 -	
Total Income		1 0 0 0 -
Expenses		
Rent Expense	6 0 0 -	
Telephone Expense	3 8 -	
Truck Expense	6 5 -	
Total Expenses		7 0 3 -
Net Income		2 9 7 -

The foregoing is an Income Statement for a nontrading, *personal-service* type of business enterprise. You will note it follows the simple formula, Total income minus total expenses equals net income.

The Income Statement for a *merchandising business* is generally a little more involved, and goes into much more detail than the one we have just seen. It is customary to divide this type of Income Statement into at least three sections. The first section shows the *gross profit on sales*; the second section shows the *total operating expenses*; and the third section shows the *net income, or net profit.* Remember, the Income Statement provides the foregoing information for a specified period of time, such as for the preceding month, or for the preceding quarter, or the preceding year.

FIRST SECTION OF INCOME STATEMENT

As stated above, the first section shows the *gross profit on sales.* The formula for finding this amount is: Net sales minus cost of goods sold equals gross profit on sales. *Net sales* means actual gross sales less sales returns, if any. If there were no sales returns, the Sales account on the Trial Balance shows the net sales. The cost of goods sold is calculated by the following formula: Merchandise inventory beginning of period plus net purchases equals merchandise available for sale less merchandise inventory end of period equals cost of goods sold.

Following the above formula line for line, this portion of the Income Statement would appear as follows:

Beginning inventory	$42,000
Plus Purchases	190,000
Merchandise available for sale	232,000
Less ending inventory	46,000
Cost of goods sold	186,000

Since the cost of goods sold is used in finding the gross profit on sales, the above portion of the statement would be included in the first of the three sections of the statement. The following is a typical Income Statement for a merchandising business.

```
                       Income Statement
                    For Month Ended June 30

  Operating income
    Sales                              250,000
    Net Sales                                       250,000

  Cost of goods sold:
    Beginning inventory                 42,000
    Plus Purchases                     190,000
    Merchandise available for sale     232,000
    Less ending inventory               46,000
    Cost of goods sold                              186,000

  Gross profit on sales                              64,000

  Operating expenses
    Rent expense                         9,600
    Telephone expense                      650
    Advertising expense                  8,500
    Salary expense                      26,000
  Total operating expenses                           44,750
    Net income (Net profit)                          19,250
```

If you will study the extended figures in the right-hand column above, you will see that the formula for finding the net income is: Net sales minus cost of goods sold equals gross profit on sales minus total operating expenses equals the net income. The formula for finding the cost of goods sold is explained at the bottom of the preceding page and the top of this page.

BASIC BOOKKEEPING EQUATION— BALANCE SHEET STATEMENT

In Lesson One we learned that although we may have as many as fifty or sixty different accounts in the general ledger, they are all divided into three groups or kinds of accounts. The three kinds of accounts are:

Asset accounts
Liability accounts
Owner's Equity accounts

Next, we learned definitions and examples of each of these three classifications. We also learned when to debit and credit each kind of account, based on the Six Fundamental Bookkeeping Rules. These were then shortened to the Three Simplified Rules. This brings us to the Basic Bookkeeping Equation, which may be expressed as follows when there are no liabilities:

$$Assets = Owner's\ Equity$$

If there are business liabilities, the equation would be expressed:

$$Assets - Liabilities = Owner's\ Equity$$

These equations can be explained, and proved, by referring to our definitions of the three kinds of accounts:

1. An Asset is anything of value owned by the business.
2. A Liability is a debt, or something we owe.
3. Owner's Equity means net worth or capital.

If we have no business liabilities, then obviously what we own equals what we are worth—or, Assets = Owner's Equity. However, if we owe on some of our possessions, then what we own minus what we owe equals what we are worth—or, Assets − Liabilities = Owner's Equity. Although we are concerned primarily with keeping the books of a business enterprise, this same equation would be true in our own personal affairs. For example, if we own clothes worth $200, furniture worth $1,200, and a car worth $3,000 (assets), and if we owe $1,400 to the bank on the car (liabilities), then we would actually be worth $3,000. Thus:

$$Assets,\ \$4,400 - Liabilities,\ \$1,400 = Owner's\ Equity,\ \$3,000$$

However, because of the usual arrangement of the *Balance Sheet Statement,* which we will discuss next, the equation is often expressed in this form:

$$Assets = Liabilities + Owner's\ Equity$$

The equation is still true, regardless of which of the two forms we express it in. This can be illustrated as follows:

Original equation	Assets, $1,000 — Liabilities, $200 = Owner's Equity, $800
Balance Sheet equation	Assets, $1,000 = Liabilities, $200 + Owner's Equity, $800

We see the equation is true, expressed in either form. Just remember, the equation derives from the fact that what we own, minus what we owe, equals what we are worth. However, because of the particular form of a Balance Sheet Statement, the equation is usually expressed this way:

Assets = Liabilities + Owner's Equity

The purpose of a Balance Sheet is to provide information regarding the status of the assets, liabilities, and owner's equity of a business as of a specified date. It is an itemized statement of the amounts of the assets, liabilities, and owner's equity at the close of business on the date indicated in the heading of the statement. The amounts are obtained from the Trial Balance taken on that same date.

Following is a Balance Sheet Statement for The Jones Co.

The Jones Co.

Balance Sheet

December 31

ASSETS		LIABILITIES	
Cash..............	1200.00	Accounts Payable......	250.00
Equipment..........	800.00		
Office Supplies....	50.00	OWNER'S EQUITY	
		Jack Jones, Capital...	1800.00
		Total liabilities	
Total assets	2050.00	and Owner's Equity	2050.00

You will note that on the left side are listed the assets of the business; on the right side are listed the liabilities and owner's equity. You will also note that the statement conforms to our equation: Assets = Liabilities + Owner's Equity.

LESSON NINE

Payroll Accounting

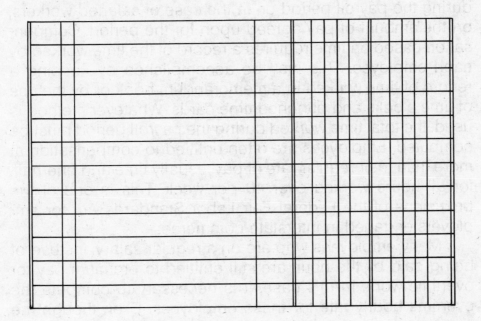

Because of the complexity of figuring and recording payroll transactions, we have purposely omitted these from the problems we have recorded to this point. In this lesson we shall now learn how to figure payrolls, how to keep payroll records, and how to journalize payroll transactions.

Employers are required by law to keep detailed and accurate payroll records. Payroll accounting records are also needed to determine the correct amount due and payable to each employee on payday.

The first step in payroll accounting is to calculate the amount of the employee's *total or gross earnings* for the pay period. The second step is to determine the amount of any *deductions* that may be required either by law or by agreement. The third step is to figure the actual *net amount* payable to each employee.

An employee's earnings are based on the time worked during the payroll period or, in the case of salaried workers, on the amount of pay agreed upon for the period. Compensation based on time requires a record of the time worked by each employee. This may be accomplished by keeping a record of time worked in a memorandum book or by the use of time clocks and punched time cards. Whatever method is used, the total time worked during the payroll period must be computed. Employees are often entitled to compensation at more than their regular rate of pay, usually time and one-half, for all hours worked over 40 per week. This is one of the provisions of the Federal Fair Labor Standards Act for employers engaged in interstate commerce.

Many employees who are on a regular salary, instead of being paid by the hour, are still entitled to premium pay for overtime work. In this case, it is necessary to compute the overtime hourly rate for these employees. Even though the employee is salaried, we would need to find the regular hourly rate and multiply that by 1½ to find the overtime hourly rate. For a person on a salary of $800 per month the overtime hourly rate would commonly be computed as follows:

$800 × 12 months = $9,600 annual pay
$9,600 divided by 52 weeks = $184.62 weekly pay
$184.62 divided by 40 hours = $4.62 regular hourly rate
$4.62 × 1½ = $6.93 *overtime hourly rate*

DEDUCTIONS FROM EARNINGS

With certain exceptions, employers are required to withhold portions of each employee's earnings for *federal income taxes* and also for *social security taxes.* Certain states and cities also require income tax withholdings by employers. In addition to these two deductions, an agreement between the employer and employee may call for other amounts to be withheld, such as for purchase of U.S. Savings Bonds, insurance premiums, and union dues.

SOCIAL SECURITY NUMBER AND FORM W-4

Each employee is required to have a social security and tax account number. Form SS-5 is the official form used in applying for this number. Each employee must furnish the employer with an Employee's Withholding Allowance Certificate, Form W-4, showing the exact number of allowances claimed, if any. The information on this form is used by the employer to help determine the amount of federal income tax to be withheld.

WITHHOLDING OF EMPLOYEES' INCOME TAX

Federal law provides that employers are required to withhold certain amounts from the total earnings of each employee, to be applied toward the payment of the employee's federal income tax. The amount to be withheld is determined by four factors: (1) the total earnings of the employee for the period, (2) the number of withholding exemptions claimed by the employee, (3) the marital status of the employee, and (4) the length of the employee's pay period. With this information, the correct amount to be withheld can be ascertained by referring to a Federal Income Tax Withholding Table furnished to employers by the Internal Revenue Service.

WITHHOLDING OF EMPLOYEES' FICA TAX

Payroll taxes are also imposed on almost all employers and emloyees under the Federal Insurance Contributions Act (FICA). This tax is generally referred to as the *old-age* or *social security tax.* In bookkeeping and accounting it is called the *FICA tax.* The amount of yearly wages taxable and the tax rate have been changed several times since the law was first enacted and are subject to change by Congress at any time in the future. For purposes of this book, a rate of 6 percent of the taxable wages paid during a calendar year will be used. The phrase *taxable wages,* as used in this book, is assumed to mean that only the first $15,000 of the wages paid to each employee in any calendar year is taxable for FICA purposes.

Many employees are unaware that in addition to the 6 percent withheld from employees' wages, the employer is required to match that amount out of his own pocket. This means when we are using a 6 percent rate, the total FICA tax that must be paid to the government by the employer for each employee is 12 percent of wages—6 percent deducted from employees' wages and 6 percent contributed by the employer.

PAYROLL REGISTER

Name	No. of Exempts.	Marital Status	Earnings					
			Hrly Rate	Tot Hrs.	O.T. Hrs.	Reg Pay	O.T. Pay	Total Pay
1. Allen, Janice	2	M	4.50	40	-	180-	-	180-
2. Brandon, Cal	1	M	5.00	44	4	200-	30-	230-
3. Cooper, Ray	3	M	6.00	40	-	240-	-	240-
Totals						620-	30-	650-

FOR PERIOD ENDED   June 30

Name	Deductions				
	FICA Tax (6%)	Fed Inc Tax	Hosp Ins	Total Ded	Net Pay
1. Allen, Janice	10.80	22.70	10.00	43.50	136.50
2. Brandon, Cal	13.80	35.70	10.00	59.50	170.50
3. Cooper, Ray	14.40	31.40	10.00	55.80	184.20
Totals	39.00	89.80	30.00	158.80	491.20

PAYROLL RECORDS

The needs of owners and managers of business enterprises and the requirements of various federal and state laws make it necessary for employers to keep payroll records that will provide pertinent information. There are three types of records that usually need to be prepared by employers. They are: (1) the payroll register, (2) the earnings record of each individual employee, and (3) the payroll check. The first of these records, the *payroll register,* is illustrated on the preceding page.

You will note the top part is the earnings section, and the bottom portion is the deductions and net pay section. The top part shows the following kinds of information for each employee: number of exemptions claimed; marital status; hourly rate of pay; total hours worked for the pay period; overtime hours, if any; regular pay; overtime pay; and total gross pay.

The bottom part shows the deductions for FICA tax, federal income tax, hospital insurance, total deductions, and net pay.

The following is a detailed explanation of the various amounts recorded for each employee on the Payroll Register.

Janice Allen's regular hourly rate is $4.50; and since she worked 40 hours, with no overtime, her regular pay is $180.00, and her total pay is $180.00 ($4.50 × 40). Her deduction for FICA tax is 6 percent of $180.00, or $10.80 (.06 × $180). The amount of her deduction for income tax is determined by using the Weekly Income Tax Withholding Table illustrated on page 134. Her deduction for hospital insurance is $10.00, by agreement. The total of the three deductions, $43.50, is subtracted from the total gross pay of $180.00 to arrive at the net pay of $136.50. The $136.50, of course, is the amount of her payroll check.

PAYROLL REGISTER

Name	No. of Exempts.	Marital Status	Earnings					
			Hrly Rate	Tot. Hrs.	O.T. Hrs.	Reg Pay	O.T Pay	Total Pay
1. Allen, Janice	2	M	4.50	40	-	180-	-	180-
2. Brandon, Cal	1	M	5.00	44	4	200-	30-	230-
3. Cooper, Ray	3	M	6.00	40	-	240-	-	240-
Totals						620-	30-	650-

FOR PERIOD ENDED   June 30

Name	Deductions				
	FICA Tax (6%)	Fed Inc Tax	Hosp Ins	Total Ded.	Net Pay
1. Allen, Janice	10.80	22.70	10.00	43.50	136.50
2. Brandon, Cal	13.80	35.70	10.00	59.50	170.50
3. Cooper, Ray	14.40	31.40	10.00	55.80	184.20
	39.00	89.80	30.00	158.80	491.20

Cal Brandon's regular hourly rate is $5.00. He worked 44 hours, which is 40 regular hours and 4 hours overtime. His regular pay is $200.00 ($5.00 × 40). His overtime hourly rate is 1½ times his regular rate ($5.00 × 1.5), or $7.50 an hour. His overtime pay is $30 ($7.50 × 4 hours). His total pay is $230.00 ($200.00 + $30.00). His deductions, which are based on his total pay of $230.00, are calculated exactly the same as the deductions for Janice Allen.

Ray Cooper's regular hourly rate is $6.00; and since he worked 40 hours, with no overtime, his regular pay is $240.00, and his total pay is $240.00 ($6.00 × 40). His deductions, which are based on his total pay of $240.00, are calculated exactly the same as the deductions for Janice Allen and Cal Brandon.

EMPLOYEE'S EARNINGS RECORD

In addition to the Payroll Register, another form called the Employee's Earnings Record is usually kept for each employee in order to provide information needed to prepare the various federal and state reports required of employers. A typical Employee's Earnings Record is illustrated below.

EMPLOYEE'S EARNINGS RECORD

For Period Ending	Earnings				Deductions				Net Pay
	Reg.	Over-time	Total	Total To Date	FICA Tax	Fed. Inc. Tax	Hosp. Ins.	Total	
6/30/77	180-	—	180-	720-	10.80	22.70	10.00	43.50	136.50
Name Position S.S. No. Ⓜ Pay $4.50 Date 6/1/77									
ALLEN, J. SEC'Y. S Rate- Employed-									

You will note this is a portion of the earnings record for Janice Allen, one of the employees listed on the Payroll Register on the preceding page. The information recorded on the record is taken from the Payroll Register. There is space at the bottom of the record to write in such information as the employee's name, position, social security number, marital status, pay rate, and date employed.

The earnings record for Janice Allen shows the pertinent information for the weekly pay period ending June 30. Actually, the record is large enough so that it contains one line for each weekly pay period in the year; thus, the earnings record is a summary of the annual earnings of the employee.

WEEKLY Payroll Period--Employee MARRIED									
And the wages are--		Number of withholding allowances claimed is--							
At least	But less than	0	1	2	3	4	5	6	7
		Amount of income tax withheld shall be--							
$125	130	18.10	15.80	13.50	11.20	8.90	6.60	4.30	2.20
130	135	18.90	16.60	14.30	12.00	9.70	7.40	5.10	2.90
135	140	19.70	17.40	15.10	12.80	10.50	8.20	5.90	3.60
140	145	20.50	18.20	15.90	13.60	11.30	9.00	6.70	4.40
145	150	21.30	19.00	16.70	14.40	12.10	9.80	7.50	5.20
150	160	22.50	20.20	17.90	15.60	13.30	11.00	8.70	6.40
160	170	24.10	21.80	19.50	17.20	14.90	12.60	10.30	8.00
170	180	26.00	23.40	21.10	18.80	16.50	14.20	11.90	9.60
→180	190	28.00	25.20	(22.70)	20.40	18.10	15.80	13.50	11.20
190	200	30.00	27.20	24.30	22.00	19.70	17.40	15.10	12.80
200	210	32.00	29.20	26.30	23.60	21.30	19.00	16.70	14.40
210	220	34.40	31.20	28.30	25.40	22.90	20.60	18.30	16.00
→230	240	39.20	(35.70)	32.30	29.40	26.50	23.80	21.50	19.20
→240	250	41.60	38.10	34.60	(31.40)	28.50	25.60	23.10	20.80
250	260	44.00	40.50	37.00	33.60	30.50	27.60	24.70	22.40

(Portion of Weekly Federal Income Tax
Withholding Table for Married Persons)

HOW TO USE INCOME TAX WITHHOLDING TABLE

On the bottom portion of the Payroll Register on page 132 we recorded the deductions for federal income taxes for each of the three employees. Reference to the Payroll Register shows the following deductions were made:

Allen, Janice—$22.70
Brandon, Cal—35.70
Cooper, Ray—31.40

These amounts were located in the withholding table in the following manner. (You will note the income tax deductions are based on the amount in the Total Pay column of the Payroll Register.) As noted on the Payroll Register, Janice Allen claimed two withholding exemptions and her total pay was $180. On the above withholding table we locate the line that reads "At least $180 but less than $190," then we move straight across to the column headed "2 withholding allowances," and we see the correct income tax is $22.70. Cal Brandon claimed one withholding exemption and his total pay was $230. On the line that reads "At least $230 but less than $240" we see that the correct tax is $35.70. Ray Cooper claimed three withholding exemptions and his total pay was $240. On the line that reads "at least $240 but less than $250" we see that the correct tax is $31.40.

Complete the following Payroll Register. You will note there are three employees listed. Complete the upper portion of the Payroll Register by computing and recording in the proper space the regular pay, overtime pay, and total pay for each employee.

HOMEWORK ASSIGNMENT NO. 11

Complete the lower portion of the Payroll Register by computing and recording in the proper space the FICA tax, the federal income tax, the total deductions, and the net pay for each employee. You will note the hospital premiums have already been recorded. In computing the federal income tax, use the withholding table on page 134.

PAYROLL REGISTER

Name	No. of Exempts.	Marital Status	Earnings					
			Hrly Rate	Tot. Hrs.	O.T. Hrs.	Reg Pay	O.T. Pay	Total Pay
1. Alton, Jane	2	M	4.50	40				
2. Banks, Carl	1	M	5.00	44	4			
3. Kane, Roy	3	M	6.00	40				

FOR PERIOD ENDED

Name	Deductions				
	FICA Tax (6%)	Fed Inc Tax	Hosp Ins	Total Ded.	Net Pay
1. Alton, Jane			10.00		
2. Banks, Carl			10.00		
3. Kane, Roy			10.00		

JOURNALIZING PAYROLL TRANSACTIONS

The Payroll Register provides the information needed to journalize the payroll transactions. In addition to the Cash account, the following accounts will be required:

Payroll Expense

This is an expense account which should be debited for the total gross wages of all employees for each pay period. Reference to the Payroll Register on page 132 shows this

Payroll Expense	
Debit	
For the total gross wages of employees for the pay period	

account should be debited for $650. Were it not for the various deductions required, recording the payroll would be relatively easy. When we pay salaries and wages we would simply debit Payroll Expense and credit Cash. Although the entry will be more complicated than that, we still debit Payroll Expense for the total wages, $650.

FICA Tax Payable

This is a liability account which should be credited for the FICA tax withheld from employees' wages, and also for the FICA tax imposed on the employer. Reference to the Payroll Re-

FICA Tax Payable	
Debit	Credit
When we pay FICA tax to the government	To record FICA taxes withheld from employees and FICA tax imposed on employer

gister on page 132 shows this account should be credited for $39. The account should be debited when we pay this tax to the government.

Employees' Income Tax Payable

This is a liability account which should be credited for the income tax withheld from employees' wages. Reference to the Payroll Register on page 132 shows this account should

Employees Income Tax Payable	
Debit	Credit
When we pay this tax to the government	To record income tax withheld from employees' wages

be credited for $89.80. The account should be debited when we pay this tax to the government.

Hospital Insurance Premiums Payable

This is a liability account which should be credited for insurance premiums withheld from employees' wages. Reference to the Payroll Register on page 132 shows this account should be credited for $30.00. The account should be debited when we send the premiums to the insurance company.

Hospital Ins. Premiums Payable	
Debit	Credit
When premiums are sent to insurance company	To record premiums withheld from employees wages

PAYROLL ENTRY IN THE GENERAL JOURNAL

Reference to the foregoing information and to the Payroll Register shows that the entry to record the payroll in the General Journal would be as follows:

	Dr.	Cr.
June 30. Payroll Expense	650.00	
FICA Tax Payable		39.00
Employees' Income Tax Payable		89.80
Hospital Ins. Premiums Payable ...		30.00
Cash		491.20

Payroll for week ended June 30

As noted on the two preceding pages, we debit Payroll Expense for the total gross wages, $650. Since we owe the government $39.00 for FICA taxes withheld, we credit the liability account FICA Tax Payable for $39.00.

Since we owe the government $89.80 for income taxes withheld, we credit the liability account Employees' Income Tax Payable for $89.80.

Since we owe the insurance company $30.00 for insurance premiums withheld, we credit the liability account Hospital Insurance Premiums Payable for $30.00.

After deducting these three amounts from the total wages of $650.00, we credit Cash for $491.20, the net amount paid to the employees. This, of course, follows Simplified Rule 1; When we pay out money, always credit Cash.

When the taxes withheld are paid to the government at the proper time, the liability accounts are debited and Cash is credited. For example, when the foregoing withholdings are sent to the government, the General Journal entry would be as follows:

```
                                        Dr.       Cr.

FICA Tax Payable ................39.00

Employees' Income Tax Payable ...89.80

   Cash ......................            128.80

Paid taxes withheld during June
```

When the insurance premiums are sent to the insurance company, the General Journal entry would be as follows:

```
Hospital Ins. Premiums Payable ... 30.00

   Cash ......................            30.00

Paid June insurance premiums
```

PAYROLL TAXES IMPOSED ON THE EMPLOYER

The foregoing taxes—FICA and federal income taxes—are taxes imposed on employees and are withheld by the employer from wages paid to employees. Such taxes are not an expense of the employer, although the employer is required by law to collect the taxes and pay them to the government.

In addition to these employee taxes, certain payroll taxes are also imposed on employers. Most employers are subject to three payroll taxes—those imposed under the Federal Insurance Contributions Act (FICA); those imposed under the Federal Unemployment Tax Act (FUTA); and those imposed under state unemployment compensation laws (State U.C. Tax).

Employer's FICA Tax

As we noted on page 137, the tax imposed under the Federal Insurance Contributions Act applies equally to employers and to employees. As previously stated, we are assuming

FICA Tax Payable

Debit	Credit
When we pay FICA tax to the government	To record *employee* ta withheld, and FICA ta imposed on *employer*

the rate to be 6 percent and that it applies only to the first $15,000 of wages paid to each employee in any calendar year. This means that 6 percent is withheld as the employee's FICA tax, and the employer contributes an additional 6 percent out of his own pocket for each employee, or a total of 12 percent. Therefore, the liability account FICA Tax Payable should be credited for both the employee and employer contributions. The account should be debited when the tax is paid to the government.

Employer's FUTA Tax

Under the Federal Unemployment Tax Act, a payroll tax is imposed on employers (but not on employees) for the purpose of aiding the states in the administration of state un-

FUTA Tax Payable

Debit	Credit
When we pay this tax to the government	To record the FUTA ta imposed on the employe

employment compensation laws. The law provides that the following employers are subject to the tax:

Employers who employ one or more individuals for at least 20 calendar weeks in the calendar year

Or who pay wages of $1,500 or more in any calendar quarter.

The tax rate has been changed by Congress from time to

time, and a credit against the levy is allowed for state unemployment taxes. In general, the federal unemployment tax rate is 3.2 percent, with a credit of 2.7 percent allowed for state unemployment taxes. This means the effective rate is 0.5 percent (3.2 percent minus 2.7 percent). This is applied to the first $4,200 of wages paid to each employee during the calendar year. Note this differs from the limitation on the FICA tax, which applies to the first $15,000 of wages paid.

The liability account FUTA Tax Payable should be credited for the tax imposed on the employer. The account should be debited when the tax is paid to the government.

State Unemployment Tax

All the states and the District of Columbia have enacted unemployment compensation laws providing for the payment of weekly benefits to qualified unemployed persons. Not all employers are subject to this tax, and there is considerable variation in the requirements from state to state. For this reason, each employer should be familiar with the unemployment compensation laws of all states in which he has one or more employees.

State Unemployment Tax Payable

Debit	Credit
When this tax is paid to the state government	To record liability for state unemployment tax on employer

For the purposes of our study we will assume the rate is 2.7 percent of the first $4,200 of wages paid to each employee. (However, under the laws of most states there is a merit rating system under which the tax rate would be less than 2.7 percent for employers who have stabilized employment. Also, in a few states employees are required to contribute, as well as employers.) The liability account State Unemployment Tax Payable should be credited for the state tax imposed on employers. The account should be debited when the tax is paid to the state government.

Payroll Tax Expense

Unlike the employee's FICA Tax and the employee's federal income tax, the foregoing three taxes are an expense of the employer. As noted above, we credit the proper liability

Payroll Tax Expense

Debit
To record FICA, FUTA, and State Unemployment Tax imposed on the employer

account for each tax and, since all three are an expense of the employer, the total of all three should be debited to the proper expense account. This account may be called Payroll Tax Expense.

JOURNALIZING EMPLOYER'S PAYROLL TAXES

The payroll taxes imposed on employers are generally recorded in the journal at the time wages are paid. Thus, the employer's liability for such taxes is then recorded in the same period as the wages on which the taxes are based. The Payroll Register on page 132 provides the information needed to ascertain the amount of payroll taxes for which the employer has become liable. The taxes are based on the figure in the Total Pay column, $650, and would be determined in the following manner:

FICA Tax, 6% of $650 (650 × .06)............$39.00
FUTA Tax, 0.5% of $650 (650 × .005)........ 3.25
State Unemployment Tax, 2.7% of $650
   (650 × .027)................................ 17.55
Total taxes...................................... 59.80

The following would be the General Journal entry to record the foregoing taxes:

                                               Dr.   Cr.

June 30. Payroll Tax Expense 59.80

           FICA Tax Payable 39.00

           FUTA Tax Payable 3.25

           State Unemployment Tax Payable ... 17.55

    To record payroll taxes imposed on employer
    with respect to wages paid June 30

Opening the Books of a New Business

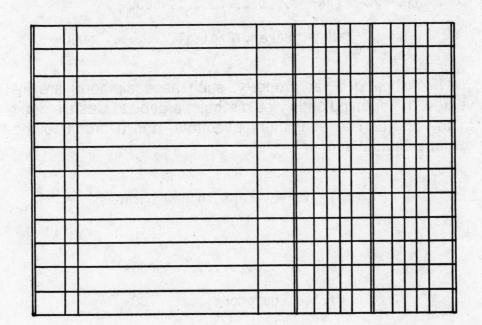

When engaging in a business enterprise as a sole owner, the owner must first decide the *amount* that he will invest and the *nature* of the property that he will invest.

The original investment may consist of cash only; or it may consist of cash and other property, such as merchandise, office equipment, and delivery equipment. Whatever property is invested should be segregated from any other property that may be owned.

After deciding on the investment to be made in the new business, the next step is to make *an opening entry in the General Journal*. If the investment consists solely of cash, the opening entry would consist of a debit to Cash and a credit to the owner's Capital account.

Example   Investment in new business

		Dr.	Cr.
Jan. 2	Cash	5000-	
	W. A. Baker, Capital		5000-

If cash *and* other property, such as equipment, are invested, the opening entry would require a debit to Cash, a debit to the appropriate equipment accounts, and a credit to the owner's Capital account.

Example   Investment in new business

		Dr.	Cr.
Jan. 2	Cash	3000-	
	Office Equipment	700-	
	Delivery Equipment ..	1000-	
	W. A. Baker, Capital		4700-

After making the opening journal entries, the owner would then open a ledger account for each of the foregoing items and post from the General Journal to the ledger accounts. After posting, the ledger accounts would look like this:

	Cash			*Delivery Equipment*	
Jan. 2	3000–		Jan. 2	1000–	

	Office Equipment			*W. A. Baker, Capital*	
Jan. 2	700–			Jan. 2	4700–

If, at the time of organizing the new business, there are any liabilities, the appropriate liability account should be credited; and the owner's Capital account should then be credited for the excess of the amount of the assets invested over the total amount of the liabilities. This, of course follows the *basic bookkeeping equation* discussed in Lesson Eight:

Assets — Liabilities = Owner's Equity

If, in the previous example, the owner owed the bank $500 on the delivery equipment he invested, the opening General Journal entry would be as follows:

Example   Investment in new business

		Dr.	Cr.
Jan. 2	Cash	3000–	
	Office Equipment	700–	
	Delivery Equipment ..	1000–	
	Accounts Payable		500–
	W. A. Baker, Capital		4200–

Notice that the assets (Cash, Office Equipment, Delivery Equipment) totaled $4700; the liabilities totaled $500. Therefore, as outlined above, the credit to W. A. Baker, Capital account was ascertained by following the basic bookkeeping equation:

Assets, $4700 — Liabilities, $500 = Owner's Equity, $4200

After posting the foregoing journal entry, the ledger accounts would look like this:

Cash

Jan. 2	3000–		

Delivery Equipment

Jan. 2	1000–		

Office Equipment

Jan. 2	700–		

Accounts Payable

		Jan. 2	500–

W. A. Baker, Capital

		Jan. 2	4200–

Answers
To Homework
Assignments

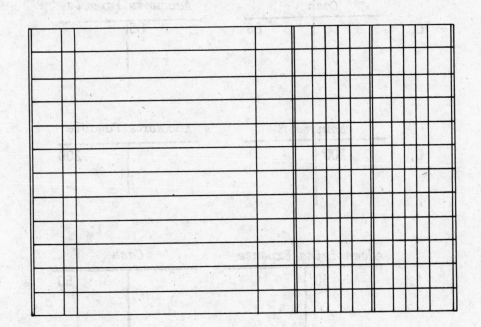

No. 1

A.

Equipment		Cash	
300			300

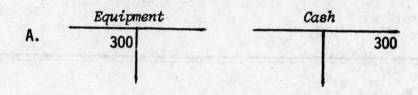

B.

Cash		Income From Fees	
60			60

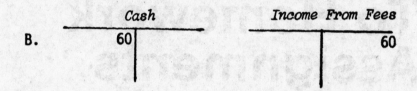

C.

Cash		Accounts Payable	
	85	85	

D.

Equipment		Accounts Payable	
200			200

E.

Advertising Expense		Cash	
50			50

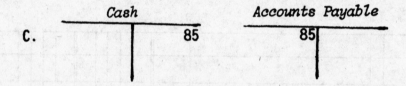

No. 2

	Cash		
(C)	60	(A)	500
(F)	80	(B)	400
		(D)	35
		(H)	38
		(I)	800
		(J)	100

Rent Expense	
(A)	500

Office Equipment	
(B)	400
(E)	125
(G)	175

Telephone Expense	
(D)	35

Accounts Payable			
(J)	100	(E)	125
		(G)	175

Electric Expense	
(H)	38

Income From Fees			
		(C)	60
		(F)	80

Salary Expense	
(I)	800

NO. 3

Jan	2	Cash	7000	-		
		James Jones, Capital			7000	-
		Investment in business				
	3	Rent Expense	500	-		
		Cash			500	-
		Paid Jan. rent				
	6	Office Equipment	200	-		
		Cash			200	-
		Purch new desk				
	10	Cash	600	-		
		Income From Fees			600	-
		Received for services				
	12	Telephone Expense	41	-		
		Cash			41	-
		Paid tel. bill				
	14	Office Equipment	560	-		
		Accounts Payable			560	-
		Bought on account				
	17	Cash	400	-		
		Income From Fees			400	-
		Received for services				
	20	Truck Expense	75	-		
		Cash			75	-
		Repairs on truck				
	21	Accounts Payable	260	-		
		Cash			260	-
		Paid on account				

NO. 4

RAY BROWN CO. - GENERAL LEDGER

Cash			No. 11
Jan 1.	6000-	Jan 2	700-
9	900-	6	300-
19	900-	11	73-
		21	41-
		26	250-

Income From Fees		No. 41
	Jan 9	900-
	19	900-

Office Equipment		No. 12
Jan 6.	300-	
16	550-	

Rent Expense		No. 51
Jan 2	700-	

Accounts Payable			No. 21
Jan 26	250-	Jan 16	550-

Telephone Expense		No. 52
Jan 11	73-	

Ray Brown, Capital		No. 31
	Jan 1.	6000-

Truck Expense		No. 53
Jan 21	41-	

NO. 5

General Ledger
Bill Barnes, Architect

Cash			No. 11		
Jan 1		3000	Jan 2		500
10		300	6		400
17	2475-	300 3600-	12		52
			20		73
			21		100
					1125-

Income From Fees		No. 41
	Jan 10	300
	17	300
		600-

Office Equipment		No. 12
Jan 6	400	
14	350	
	750-	

Rent Expense		No. 51
Jan 2	500	

Accounts Payable			No. 21
Jan 21	100	Jan 14 250-	350

Telephone Expense		No. 52
Jan 12	52	

Bill Barnes, Capital		No. 31
	Jan 1	3000

Electric Expense		No. 53
Jan 20	73	

Bill Barnes, Architect
Trial Balance
January 31

	Debit				Credit			
Cash	2	4	7	5	-				
Office Equipment		7	5	0	-				
Accounts Payable							2	5	0	-
Bill Barnes, Capital						3	0	0	0	-
Income From Fees							6	0	0	-
Rent Expense		5	0	0	-				
Telephone Expense			5	2	-				
Electric Expense			7	3	-				
	3	8	5	0	-	3	8	5	0	-

NO. 6

Date	Description	P.F.	Debit	Credit
May 1	Cash		7000 -	
	Joe Cross, Capital			7000 -
	Investment in business			
2	Rent Expense		600 -	
	Cash			600 -
	Paid May rent			
5	Cash		650 -	
	Dry Cleaning Income			650 -
	Received for services			
8	Dry Clean. Equipment		1200 -	
	Accounts Payable			1200 -
	Bought on account			
12	Telephone Expense		42 -	
	Cash			42 -
	Paid tel. bill			
18	Cash		850 -	
	Dry Cleaning Income			850 -
	Received for services			
20	Advertising Expense		85 -	
	Cash			85 -
	Paid Daily Post			
22	Dry Clean. Equipment		600 -	
	Accounts Payable			600 -
	Bought on account			
28	Accounts Payable		300 -	
	Cash			300 -
	Paid on account			

Cash			No. 11
May 1	7000-	May 2	600-
5	650-	12	42 -
18	850-	20	85-
7473 *8500*		28	300-
			1627-

Dry Cleaning Income			No. 41
		May 5	650-
		18	850-
			1500-

Dry Cleaning Equipment		No. 12
May 8	1200-	
22	600-	
	1800-	

Rent Expense		No. 51
May 2	600-	

Accounts Payable			No. 21
May 28	300-	May 8	1200-
		22	600-
		1500-	*1800-*

Telephone Expense		No. 52
May 12	42-	

Joe Cross, Capital			No. 31
		May 1	7000-

Advertising Expense		No. 53
May 20	85-	

NO. 6 CONTINUED

Joe Cross Cleaners

Trial Balance

					Dr.						Cr.
Cash		7	4	7	3	-					
Dry Cleaning Equipment		1	8	0	0	-					
Accounts Payable								1	5	0	0	-
Joe Cross, Capital								7	0	0	0	-
Dry Cleaning Income								1	5	0	0	-
Rent Expense			6	0	0	-					
Telephone Expense				4	2	-					
Advertising Expense				8	5	-					
		10	0	0	0	-		10	0	0	0	-

NO. 7

CASH				Date	Description	P R	GENERAL			
Debit		Credit					Debit		Credit	
		700-		Jan 1	Rent Expense		700-			
	30-			5	Income From Fees				30-	
				7	Office Equipment		400-			
					Accounts Payable				400-	
		200-		9	Accounts Payable		200-			
	30-	900-					1300-		430-	

Proof Of Footings

Cash Debit	30-		Cash Credit	900-
General Debit	1300-		General Credit	430-
Total	1330-		Total	1330

Cash	No. 11	Accounts Payable	No. 21
Jan 31 30-	Jan 31 900-	Jan 9 200-	Jan 7 400-

Office Equipment	No. 12	Income From Fees	No. 41
Jan 7 400-			Jan 5 30-

		Rent Expense	No. 51
		Jan 1 700-	

NO. 8

Date	Description	P.F.	Debit	Credit
Jul 1	Cash		1000 -	
	Jim Carter, Capital			1000 -
	Initial investment			
2	Rent Expense		700 -	
	Cash			700 -
	Paid July rent			
3	Purchases		80 -	
	Cash			80 -
	Bought merchandise			
9	Office Equipment		250 -	
	Accounts Payable			250 -
	Bought on account			

Purchases Journal

Date	Inv.	From Whom Purchased	Amount
Jul 5	2	Kane Co.	200 -
7	3	Goss Co.	300 -
31		Dr. Purch. & Cr. Accts. Pay.	500 -

POSTING

Post *each* amount from the General Journal to the ledger accounts below. Then, post just the *total* from the Purchases Journal. Remember, the total of the Purchases Journal is posted to *two accounts* in the ledger.

Cash			*No. 11*
Jul 1	1000-	Jul 2	700-
		3	80-

Jim Carter, Capital			*No. 31*
		Jul 1	1000-

Office Equipment			*No. 12*
Jul 9	250-		

Purchases			*No. 51*
Jul 3	80-		

Accounts Payable			*No. 21*
		Jul 9	250-

Rent Expense			*No. 61*
Jul 2	700-		

The Carter Co. - Trial Balance

Accounts	Debit	Credit
Cash	220 -	
Office Equipment	250 -	
Accounts Payable		250 -
Jim Carter, Capital		1000 -
Purchases	580 -	
Rent Expense	700 -	
	1250 -	1250 -

NO. 9

Record the following June transactions for The Dodge Co. in the two journals below. Enter all charge sales in the Sales Journal; enter all other transactions, including cash sales, in the General Journal.

Jun 1. Joe Dodge invested $4000 in a new business

Jun 2. Paid June rent, $900

Jun 3. Sold merch. for cash, $200, sales tax $8.00

Jun 4. Sold merch. on account to J. S. Brown, $300, sales tax $12.00

Jun 5. Sold merch. on account to A. B. Fuller, $400, sales tax $16.00

Date		Description	P.F.	Debit	Credit
Jun	1	Cash	11	4000 –	
		Joe Dodge, Capital	31		4000 –
		Investment in business			
	2	Rent Expense	61	900 –	
		Cash	11		900 –
		Paid June rent			
	3	Cash	11	208 –	
		Sales	41		200 –
		Sales Tax Payable	22		8 –
		Cash sales			

Date	Sale No.	To Whom Sold	PF	Accounts Rec. Dr.	Sales Cr.	Sales Tax Payable Cr.
Jun 4	1	J.S. Brown		312 –	300 –	12 –
5	2	A. B. Fuller		416 –	400 –	16 –
30		*Totals*		728 –	700 –	28 –

Post *every figure* from the General Journal to the ledger accounts below. Then post the three totals from the Sales Journal as indicated by the column headings. Use the June 30 date when posting the totals.

Cash		*No. 11*
Jun 1	4000-	Jun 2　900-
3	208-	
3308-	4208-	

Joe Dodge, Capital		*No. 31*
		Jun 1　4000-

Accounts Receivable		*No. 12*
Jun 30	728-	

Sales		*No. 41*
		Jun 3　200-
		30　700-
		900-

Sales Tax Payable		*No. 22*
		Jun 3　8-
		30　28-
		36-

Rent Expense		*No. 61*
Jun 2	900-	

TRIAL BALANCE

Foot each ledger account and find the balance for each account; then, list each account and its balance on the Trial Balance form below. (See *Pages 38–40*.)

The Dodge Co.
Trial Balance

Accounts	Debit	Credit
Cash	3308 -	
Accounts Receivable	728 -	
Sales Tax Payable		36 -
Joe Dodge, Capital		4000 -
Sales		900 -
Rent Expense	900 -	
	4936 -	4936 -

NO. 10

Jul 1. Owner invested $6000 cash in new business.

Jul 1. Paid July rent $900

Jul 2. Purchased merch. on account from Grimes Co. $700

Jul 3. Sold merch. on account to B. A. Hall, sales $100, tax $4.00

Jul 5. Purchased merchandise for cash $800

Jul 7. Sold merch. for cash, sales $200, tax $8.00

Jul 15. Purchased merch. on account from Hames Co. $400

Jul 17. Purchased new office desk from Lane Co. on account $300

Jul 22. Sold merch. on account to Jay Reed, sale $400, tax $16.00

Jul 23. Paid Grimes Co. $200 on account

Jul 28. Paid electric bill $78

Jul 30. Received $104 cash on account from P. A. Hall

PURCHASES JOURNAL

Date		Inv.	From Whom Purchased		Amount	
Jul	2	1	Grimes Co.		700	-
	15	2	Hames Co.		400	-
	31		Dr. Purch & Cr. Accounts Pay.		1100	-

Combined Cash Journal   For Month Of *July*

Cash Dr.	Cash Cr.	Day	Description	P R	General Dr.	General Cr.	Accounts Pay. Dr.	Accounts Rec. Cr.	Sales Cr.	Sales Tx Pay. Cr.
6000-		1	Wayne Walker, Capital			6000-				
	900-	1	Rent Expense		900-					
	800-	5	Purchases		800-					
208-		7	Cash sales						200-	8-
		17	Office Equipment		300-					
			Accounts Payable			300-				
	200-	23	Grimes Co.				200-			
	78-	28	Electric Expense		78-					
104-		30	B.A. Hall					104-		
6312-	1978-	31	*Totals*		2078-	6300-	200-	104-	200-	8-

Date	Sale No.	To Whom Sold	P F	Accounts Rec. Dr.	Sales Cr.	Sales Tax Payable Cr.
Jul 3	1	B.A. Hall		104-	100-	4-
22	2	Jay Reed		416-	400-	16-
31		*Totals*		520-	500-	20-

THE WALKER STORE GENERAL LEDGER ACCOUNTS

Cash No. 11

| Jul 31 | 6312- | Jul 31 | 1978- |

Accounts Receivable No. 12

| Jul 31 | 520- | Jul 31 | 104- |

Office Equipment No. 14

| Jul 17 | 300- | | |

Accounts Payable No. 21

| Jul 31 | 200- | Jul 17 | 300- |
| | | 31 | 1100- |

Sales Tax Payable No. 22

| Jul 31 | 8- | | |
| 31 | 20- | | |

Wayne Walker, Capital No. 31

| | | Jul 1 | 6000- |

Sales No. 41

| | | Jul 31 | 200- |
| | | 31 | 500- |

Purchases No. 51

| Jul 5 | 800- | | |
| 31 | 1100- | | |

Rent Expense No. 61

| Jul 1 | 900- | | |

Electric Expense No. 63

| Jul 28 | 78- | | |

POSTING—Total all three journals and prove the footings of the Combined Cash Journal and the Sales Journal. Then, post from the three journals to the ledger accounts on this page. *(Refer to Page 90).*

THE TRIAL BALANCE

After posting from the three journals to the ledger accounts, foot the ledger accounts and find the balance for each account. Enter the balance on the larger side of each account. *(Refer to Pages 38, 39, & 40.)* Take a Trial Balance on the form below.

THE WALKER STORE
TRIAL BALANCE
JULY 31

Account	Debit	Credit
Cash	4 3 3 4 —	
Accounts Receivable	4 1 6 —	
Office Equipment	3 0 0 —	
Accounts Payable		1 2 0 0 —
Sales Tax Payable		2 8 —
Wayne Walker, Capital		6 0 0 0 —
Sales		7 0 0 —
Purchases	1 9 0 0 —	
Rent Expense	9 0 0 —	
Electric Expense	7 8 —	
	7 9 2 8 —	7 9 2 8 —

NO. 11

Complete the following Payroll Register. You will note there are three employees listed. Complete the upper portion of the Payroll Register by computing and recording in the proper space the regular pay, overtime, and total pay for each employee.

Complete the lower portion of the Payroll Register by computing and recording in the proper space the FICA tax, the federal income tax, the total deductions, and the net pay for each employee. You will note the hospital premiums have already been recorded. In computing the federal income tax use the withholding table on *Page 119*.

PAYROLL REGISTER

Name	No. of Exempts.	Marital Status	Earnings					
			Hrly Rate	Tot. Hrs.	O.T. Hrs.	Reg Pay	O.T. Pay	Total Pay
1. Alton, Jane	2	M	4.50	40		180		180
2. Banks, Carl	1	M	5.00	44	4	200	30	230
3. Kane, Roy	3	M	6.00	40		240		240

FOR PERIOD ENDED

Name	Deductions				
	FICA Tax (6%).	Fed Inc Tax	Hosp Ins	Total Ded.	Net Pay
1. Alton, Jane	10.80	22.70	10.00	43.50	136.50
2. Banks, Carl	13.80	35.70	10.00	59.50	170.50
3. Kane, Roy	14.40	31.40	10.00	55.80	184.20
	39.00	89.80	30.00	158.80	491.20